CONTEMPORARY WRITERS

General Editors
MALCOLM BRADBURY
and
CHRISTOPHER BIGSBY

RICHARD BRAUTIGAN

IN THE SAME SERIES

Donald Barthelme   *M. Couturier and R. Durand*
Saul Bellow   *Malcolm Bradbury*
John Fowles   *Peter Conradi*
Seamus Heaney   *Blake Morrison*
Philip Larkin   *Andrew Motion*
Doris Lessing   *Lorna Sage*
Joe Orton   *C. W. E. Bigsby*
Harold Pinter   *G. Almansi and S. Henderson*
Thomas Pynchon   *Tony Tanner*
Philip Roth   *Hermione Lee*
Kurt Vonnegut   *Jerome Klinkowitz*

RICHARD
BRAUTIGAN

MARC CHENETIER

METHUEN
LONDON AND NEW YORK

First published in 1983 by
Methuen & Co. Ltd
11 New Fetter Lane, London EC4P 4EE
Published in the USA by
Methuen & Co.
in association with Methuen, Inc.
733 Third Avenue, New York, NY 10017

Typeset by Rowland Phototypesetting Ltd
Printed in Great Britain by
Richard Clay (The Chaucer Press) Ltd
Bungay, Suffolk

British Library Cataloguing in Publication Data

Chénetier, Marc
Richard Brautigan.—(Contemporary writers)
1. Brautigan, Richard—Criticism and
interpretation
I. Title   II. Series
813'.54   PS3053.R2736Z/
ISBN 0-416-32960-8

Library of Congress Cataloging in Publication Data

Chénetier, Marc, 1946–
Richard Brautigan.
(Contemporary writers)
Bibliography: p.
1. Brautigan, Richard—Criticism and interpretation.
I. Title.   II. Series.
PS3503.R2736Z6   1983   813'.54   82-20880
ISBN 0-416-32960-8 (pbk.)

For Peter Brown,
who made me read,
and
André Le Vot,
who made me write

CONTENTS

	General editors' preface	8
	Acknowledgements	11
	A note on the texts	13
1	Censors and censers, minors and miners	15
2	Entrapments and liberations	21
3	The driftwood artist	40
4	Libraries and laboratories: a gallery of monsters	52
5	Strip(under)mining	65
6	The reel world	79
	Notes	93
	Bibliography	95

GENERAL EDITORS' PREFACE

Over the past twenty years or so, it has become clear that a decisive change has taken place in the spirit and character of contemporary writing. There now exists around us, in fiction, drama and poetry, a major achievement which belongs to our experience, our doubts and uncertainties, our ways of perceiving – an achievement stylistically radical and novel, and likely to be regarded as quite as exciting, important and innovative as that of any previous period. This is a consciousness and a confidence that has grown very slowly. In the 1950s it seemed that, somewhere amidst the dark realities of the Second World War, the great modernist impulse of the early years of this century had exhausted itself, and that the post-war arts would be arts of recessiveness, pale imitation, relative sterility. Some, indeed, doubted the ability of literature to survive the experiences of holocaust. A few major figures seemed to exist, but not a style or a direction. By the 1960s the confidence was greater, the sense of an avant-garde returned, the talents multiplied, and there was a growing hunger to define the appropriate styles, tendencies and forms of a new time. And by the 1970s it was not hard to see that we were now surrounded by a remarkable, plural, innovative generation, indeed several layers of generations, whose works represented a radical inquiry into contemporary forms and required us to read and understand – or, often, to read and *not* understand – in quite new ways. Today, as the 1980s start, that cumulative post-war achievement has acquired a degree of coherence that allows for critical response and understanding; hence the present series.

We thus start it in the conviction that the age of Beckett, Borges, Nabokov, Bellow, Pynchon, Robbe-Grillet, Golding, Murdoch, Fowles, Grass, Handke and Calvino, of Albee, Mamet, Shepard, Ionesco, Orton, Pinter and Stoppard, of Ginsberg, Lowell, Ashbery, Paz, Larkin and Hughes, and many another, is indeed an outstanding age of international creation, striking experiment, and some degree of aesthetic coherence. It is a time that has been described as 'post-modern', in the sense that it is an era consequent to modernism yet different from it, having its own distinctive preoccupations and stylistic choices. That term has its limitations, because it is apt to generate too precise definitions of the contemporary experiment, and has acquired rather too specific associations with contemporary American writing; but it does help concentrate our sense of living in a distinctive period. With the new writing has come a new criticism or rather a new critical theorem, its thrust being 'structuralist' or 'deconstructive' − a theorem that not only coexists with but has affected that writing (to the point where many of the best theorists write fictions, the best fictionalists write criticism). Again, its theory can be hermetic and enclosing, if not profoundly apocalyptic; but it points to the presence in our time of a new sense of the status of word and text, author and reader, which shapes and structures the making of modern form.

The aim of 'Contemporary Writers' is to consider some of the most important figures in this scene, looking from the standpoint of and at the achievement of the writers themselves. Its aims are eclectic, and it will follow no tight definition of the contemporary; it will function on the assumption that contemporary writing is by its nature multidirectional and elusive, since styles and directions keep constantly changing in writers who, unlike the writers of the past, are continuous, incomplete, not dead (though several of these studies will address the careers of those who, though dead, remain our contemporaries, as many of those who continue to write are manifestly not). A fair criticism of living writers must be assertive but also provisional, just as a fair sense of contemporary style must be open to that most crucial of contemporary awarenesses, that of the suddenness of change. We do not assume, then, that there is one right path to contemporary experiment, nor that a self-conscious reflexiveness, a deconstructive strategy, an art of performance or a metafictional mode is the only one of current importance. As Iris Murdoch said, 'a strong agile realism which is of course not photographic naturalism' – associated perhaps especially with British writing, but also with Latin-American and American – is also a major component of modern style.

So in this series we wish to identify major writers, some of whom are avant-garde, others who are familiar, even popular, but all of whom are in some serious sense contemporary and in some contemporary sense serious. The aim is to offer brief, lucid studies of their work which draw on modern theoretical issues but respond, as much modern criticism does not, to their distinctiveness and individual interest. We have looked for contributors who are engaged with their subjects – some of them being significant practising authors themselves, writing out of creative experience, others of whom are critics whose interest is personal as well as theoretical. Each volume will provide a thorough account of the author's work so far, a solid bibliography, a personal judgement – and, we hope, an enlarged understanding of writers who are important, not only because of the individual force of their work, but because they are ours in ways no past writer could really be.

Norwich, England   MALCOLM BRADBURY
                                CHRISTOPHER BIGSBY

ACKNOWLEDGEMENTS

I am grateful to the following magazines which published, in French, my previous articles on Brautigan: *Caliban* (Toulouse), *Trema, La Revue Française d'Études Américaines* and *Les Cahiers de l'Herne* (all from Paris), and *The Stanford French Review* (USA). Excerpts from these studies appear in modified form in this book. Likewise, fragments of a piece appearing in *Les Cahiers de Fontenay* are drawn on for the final chapter.

For their trust and courtesy, André Le Vot, Maurice Lévy, Marc Bertrand and Catherine Vieilledent have my gratitude; the work done on Brautigan by M. C. Agosto, Lisa Zucker and many of my students over the years has proved most stimulating, and I wish to thank them here. Helen Brann, Richard Brautigan's literary agent, has been very helpful; and I am also grateful to Malcolm Bradbury, Christopher Bigsby and Linden Stafford for their skilful part in the abridgement of the English text.

Finally, there are gestures of friendship and trust which writers do not have to make to their critics. But Richard Brautigan made them: and, for emboldening me, and making firmer my insecure intuitions, my warmest thanks and friendship go out to him. How *does* one thank anybody for ten years of happy reading?

The author and publisher would like to thank the following for permission to reproduce copyright material: Richard Brautigan, Dell Publishing Co., Inc. and Jonathan Cape Ltd for extracts from *Trout Fishing in America* and *In Watermelon Sugar*.

Paris, 1982   MARC CHENETIER

A NOTE ON THE TEXTS

Page references to quotations from Richard Brautigan's work are taken from the editions listed below. The following abbreviations have been used:

CG   *A Confederate General from Big Sur* (New York: Grove, 1964)

TFA   *Trout Fishing in America* (New York: Dell/Laurel, 1967)

IWS   *In Watermelon Sugar* (New York: Dell/Delta, 1968)

RL   *Revenge of the Lawn* (New York: Pocket Books, 1972)

A   *The Abortion* (New York: Simon & Schuster/ Touchstone, 1971)

HM   *The Hawkline Monster* (New York: Simon & Schuster, 1974)

WBT   *Willard and his Bowling Trophies* (New York: Simon & Schuster, 1974)

SF   *Sombrero Fallout* (New York: Simon & Schuster, 1976)

DB   *Dreaming of Babylon* (New York: Delacorte Press/ Seymour Lawrence, 1977)

TME   *The Tokyo–Montana Express* (New York: Delacorte Press/Seymour Lawrence, 1980)

Pill   *The Pill Versus the Springhill Mine Disaster* (New York: Dell/Delta, 1968)

Rommel   *Rommel Drives on Deep into Egypt* (New York: Dell/Delta, 1970)

LMP   *Loading Mercury with a Pitchfork* (New York: Simon & Schuster/Touchstone, 1976)

J30   *June 30th–June 30th* (New York: Dell/Delta, 1978)

1

CENSORS AND CENSERS,
MINORS AND MINERS

As for me, if I were asked what Anna Karenina was about, I
would have to write the book all over again. (Leo Tolstoy)

Ever since Richard Brautigan's remarkable irruption on to the
experimental, radical literary scene of the mid-1960s, his work
has come in for much the same kind of commentary. A poet
who had been hovering discreetly on the edges of the fifties Beat
Generation while he was in his twenties (Richard Brautigan
was born in 1935, in Tacoma, Washington) had now made it
on his own, and emerged as the product-image-leader of the
Woodstock-generation sensibility. Firmly anchored, therefore,
amid the rolling fleet of sixties personalities – Hermann Hesse,
Carlos Castañeda, Alvin Toffler, Charles Reich – Brautigan
could then be celebrated or damned, according to the view one
took of the whole 'hippie' tendency. His work could be praised
for its 'gentle' and 'zany' qualities, or else condemned for its
trendiness or naïveté. It is difficult for any writer, when he is
perched astride two self-conscious generations, in a culture
highly sensitive to fashion and eager for period pieces, not to
become completely a product of his times; and this happened
to Brautigan.

No one can deny that Brautigan's first four works of fiction
stood as strong, eerie harmonics of a time when America was
supposed to be 'greening', when a new mood of questioning
prevailed, and youth was 'in'. Nor was Brautigan averse to
endorsing a stage in his career that not only brought him great
fame but also preserved for him a modicum of the youth he had
spent in a San Francisco still more strongly flavoured with the

spirit of North Beach than that of Haight-Ashbury. All this was a powerful and popular characterization for its time, but it was always insufficient. The peculiar, radical kind of writing which was, from the start, Brautigan's hallmark cannot, and should never have been, reduced to a set of vapid social themes, or an innocent plucking of leaves away from what Pierre-Yves Pétillon calls 'the artichoke heart of the Woodstock generation'. Moreover, Brautigan's career certainly did not end when the social phenomenon he was supposed to express subsided and the sixties turned into something else. In fact, it has gone on to display even more clearly the originality and the genuine contribution of a fiction writer who – as this book will argue – has always been much more akin to the metafictionists of the seventies than to the naïve flower-children of what I should like to call the pre-Nixapsarian sixties.

Certainly, though, as long as Brautigan's productions were still limited to the early poems (ending with *The Pill Versus the Springhill Mine Disaster* (1968) and *Rommel Drives on Deep into Egypt* (1970)) and to his first four novels (*A Confederate General from Big Sur* (1964), *Trout Fishing in America* (1967), *In Watermelon Sugar* (1968) and *The Abortion* (1971)), it could remain plausible – if not very satisfactory – to ignore the specific technical qualities of a highly experimental writer, and instead invest all one's critical capital in the study of his themes and subject-matter, or else set out in quest of the elusive, whimsical, half-hidden first-person narrator who seemed to stare out from the book covers in the guise of a John-Lennon-like idol. There was a strong body of cultural and social phenomena to turn to on the one hand, a seemingly weird author-as-personality on the other; the path towards critical label-mongering was more or less irresistible. So, by the seventies, when the time came for the academics to stand back and take stock, most of the critical studies that appeared in the USA were written in a haze of nostalgia or cultural evocation. They drew their arguments from past debates and decisions, calling up the lore of 'relevance and grooviness', all the nickel-and-dime cultural and metaphysical interrogations that invaded the sixties classrooms, and the columns of both the *Berkeley Barb* and *Time* magazine. Brautigan's own complexion and complexity apparently would not suffice; study after study gave evidence of what Roland Barthes used to call 'cosmetic' criticism. Naming was solving: 'funky' and 'young' became part of the critical vocabulary. At best Brautigan was disliked and dismissed, locked into that category reserved for 'minor' writers who have caught a mood or become a phenomenon. At worst he was venerated, covered from famed sombrero to surmised cowboy boot-tip with vague and empty adulation. In the end any censer kills, smothers and censors the iconic object much more surely than does total silence. Criticism becomes incantation; the author is masked and concealed by his followers.

Since then, this approach largely having had its day, it has mainly been replaced by what Cleanth Brooks used to call 'the heresy of paraphrase'. Criticism retells the matter of his work but loses sight of its essential spirit; no explanations are offered of the unique blend of inventions and devices that gives his fictions their particular and extraordinary flavour. Moreover, when Brautigan began to publish books that no longer fitted his received image, critical activity largely responded by discarding him. His next four novels were mostly panned by their reviewers; the celebrated 'easy vignettes' ('easy' as in 'easy rider' or 'five easy pieces'), which carried their all-important message to the sixties, were now read as merely easy in the sense of facile, and could therefore be readily discarded. Little attention was paid to the potential aesthetic pertinence of a fragmentary, self-questioning experimental activity, equivalents of which were in the meantime warmly praised when they came from the pen of Donald Barthelme, writing in the *New Yorker*. The sixties had taken its arts from the communes and the country; apparently the seventies and eighties had moved right back into town, among the condominiums, and our author had not. If criticism of Brautigan turned to anything now, it was to his themes, but with a similar poverty of discussion. The life-asserting, free-floating, liberated, funny hippie of the sixties was increasingly credited with a darkening vision, but this was just seen as another phenomenon of cultural history; the times they were a-changing. Brautigan was gradually discovered to be obsessed with the duality of an existence irretrievably divided between (as the critics liked to say) life and death, but these shadows in his work – though in fact they had always been there for the finding – were simply read as proof that the light of the sixties had faded into the night of the seventies. This explained why their primary mouthpiece had grown sour, sad and gloomy. No one, still, cared to examine the craft of a writer whose continuing work made him ever harder to parody and deride; in the accepted view, Brautigan was the voice of an era that had come and gone, his poems were mere nothings, and his prose was increasingly vacuous and 'irrelevant'.

It is not the purpose of this study to claim that Brautigan rivals Melville and Faulkner, that his trout dwarfs the white whale or his Confederate general outflanks the Sartorises. Neither do I plan to dismiss all thematic approaches to his work. However, the 'minor' status Brautigan is now accorded seems ridiculously inadequate if one is convinced, as much of the best Western criticism of the past thirty years has been, that, as Harry Levin put it in 1950, 'technicalities help us more than generalities'.[1] Brautigan's misfortune is that he lost out on two counts: those who were really interested in his work have wielded either outdated or naïve critical weapons, while those with more sophisticated and useful tools of analysis have not chosen to concern themselves with a writer judged to be of slender repute and slight status. In a time when fiction writers have been increasingly pressed to make ponderous statements on the origin, nature, problems and future (if any) of fiction, Brautigan has never given a single long interview on his craft or ideas. He has tended to mock his own endeavours, refusing to take them as seriously as serious writers are expected to do. He has displayed in his work an undoubted irreverence for critical institutions, but without asserting that aggressive anti-intellectualism that would locate him in a time-honoured

18

American literary tradition. For such reasons, Brautigan has been identified as a 'minor' writer; but other, more specifically literary, reasons have been advanced for regarding him in that light. An apparent thematic thinness has alienated philosophically inclined critics, while his very popularity has repelled many serious critical analysts. More classical critics have been disturbed by the gradual disappearance from his work both of predictable content and of traditionally dominant features of the novel (plot, character, setting); while his lack of explicit theoretical assertion has not won him the interest of those concerned with innovative developments in American fiction. Oddly placed, then, on the margins of 'metafiction' and 'postmodernism' (margins being where Brautigan likes to be), he has not been given full admission into that club – or, rather, as John Barth has so nicely put it, been 'clubbed into admission'.[2]

So, at a time when the most theoretically interesting American writers have far more articles written about them than they have copies sold of their books, and when dubious bestsellers keep on bestselling despite their meagre literary qualities, this most contemporary of American writers sells millions of intelligently crafted books to engaged audiences in the midst of a near-total critical silence. Perhaps Brautigan is in fact so easily read that it is perverse to look for the intricate complexities of his craftsmanship. Certainly few have felt inclined to explore the inner workings of texts which are, on the surface, so easily 'consumed', even though they obviously resist traditional approaches. But, as I have tried to explain elsewhere,[3] it is not only what Osip Brik called 'literary generals' who make for the advance of literature, and an assessment of Brautigan's contribution seems in order at the precise moment when public interest shows some signs of flagging, and the artificial nature of his reputation is beginning to fade. Detailed analyses of Brautigan's fiction are so few and far between that there are no lances to be tilted at anyone. Apart from the few stimulating theoretical discussions of his work which do exist (Tanner, Pétillon and Pütz, in particular), there is really a large critical desert.

There exists – at least in the world of jokes – a method of lion-hunting which involves sifting all the sands of the Sahara in order to be left with a bewildered lion or two at the bottom of the sieve. In this book, my concern is not with the lions that the thematic critics have found but with the sand itself. Story-line, period-mood and message-for-our-times lions have been dealt with long ago. For me, Brautigan, if a 'minor' writer, is a far more important miner than many recognized writers. If Boris Vian or Nathanael West are minor writers, Brautigan is indeed in very good company. There will be talk in the following chapters of drilling and digging, of explosions and under-mining, of lodes and crystals, of surfaces and refining processes – all things that are appropriate to an heir of Bret Harte and Mark Twain, a lover of the American West, an author who has written a preface to Joseph Francl's western diary.[4] Mapping out a territory is as important as settling it, and one may prefer census-taking to sense-making: the actual weighing of the nuggets will be left to others. After all, I too am just another miner, dealing with the ores and pans; the scales of individual taste are for each reader of Brautigan's works to use.

2

ENTRAPMENTS AND
LIBERATIONS

Elizabeth's voice had a door in it. When you opened that
door you found another door and that door opened yet
another door. All the doors were nice and led out of her. (*A
Confederate General from Big Sur*)

Brautigan is a writer of enormous comic powers; but there is no
doubt that one aspect of his comedy derives from the strange
sense of unease, instability and malfunction that is generated
by his books. Unless one chooses to attribute a moral value to
his nostalgic themes and their in fact very detached treatment,
it is difficult to find in his works any statements that create a
system of judgements and assessments of the real world. The
status of reality in Brautigan's novels and stories is always such
that we cannot take them straightforwardly; rather than
asserting the value of the real, these texts take their specific and
unmistakable quality from a persistent speculation on the very
nature of the real, as well as of textual activity itself. Referentiality and meaning evidently exist – but they are products,
oozing from underneath the surface of texts that are generated
in autonomous and metamorphic ways. Brautigan is a writer
concerned with defying language's fixities and points of reference; indeed, I believe all his books are motivated by one
central concern and activated by one central dialectic: they are
driven by an obsessive interrogation of the fossilization and
fixture of language, and by a counter-desire to free it from
stultification and paralysis. The genesis and the contents of his
early novels, in particular, seem clearly predicated on the
antagonism he develops between, on the one hand, fixed forms
and stabilized references and, on the other, the way these might

be fractured – through literary techniques, linguistic complications and distortions, and the workings of the imagination. This is why, in these novels, anything but a metafictional reading seems doomed to be simplistic, or else condemns the text to a lasting illegibility.

The structure of Brautigan's first published novel, *A Confederate General from Big Sur* (1964), offers numerous examples of this overall strategy; structural organization, the iconographic stock, syntax and intertextuality alike work to illustrate and deny the predicament of all literary creativity. 'A boy of sixteen, uniform torn awry like a playground in an earthquake, lay dead next to an old man of fifty-nine, uniform solemn as a church, complete, closed, dead' (*CG*, p. 125): one could no doubt read this brief vignette as a vision of the sad fate equally reserved for youthful, playfully disturbed and distorted discourse, and the more traditional and solemn discourses, dead in their 'uniformity'. Even if this reading is too metaphorical, the lexical set with which the passage ends – 'complete, closed, dead' – serves as a useful starting-point. In the three equalized adjectives is an image of fixity as sterility; all discourses are eventually bound to stall and grow paralytic, and literary activity might then consist in exposing the mechanisms by which this occurs, in exploring the ways in which they might be reactivated, in eliciting the diverse strategies we might (even if hopelessly) employ to re-endow writing with momentum and creative energy. And this, certainly, is the spirit of a novel which, pompously and deceptively, announces itself (*CG*, p. 21) as a 'military narrative' – only to proceed by amending, varying and overturning its military motifs, multiplying, complicating and transforming its original 'official' discourse.

The 'official' discourse starts in the prologue, which solemnly offers to account for the 'attrition' of the 425 Confederate generals appointed during the Civil War, and then goes on to provide us with details of their peacetime employments. This documentary listing – which neatly asserts from the start that a 'Confederate general' is always something else at the same time – makes an initial dent in the narrative potential of the title.

'Attrition' stands like a key at the beginning of the score; the numerical score itemizes the attrition itself. The 'tatters' that Lee Mellon will wear, the 'ruins' he will be in at the end of the first chapter, are thus harmonically announced. We likewise learn quickly that there was actually no such general as Augustus Mellon, the ancestor Lee Mellon claims; he does not exist in books and records, though this does not prevent him from living in the imagination of his descendant and acting as a control on the wild antics the text will perform in its claims to freedom. That freedom, a wilful violation of reality, then immediately becomes the matter of the opening chapter, when the narrator confesses his surprise at learning that Big Sur has been a member of the Confederacy, and then offers an account of the participation of the Big Sur Digger Indians in the Battle of the Wilderness. Even before the story of this alleged 'Confederate general' begins, its credibility has been jeopardized, the prologue made into pre-text, the story set free from stabilized documentation. In other words, the imaginative *coup de force* which gives the narrative its initial energy confesses straight away to its true nature: it is simply something to start from, an imaginative possibility, something bound to ride, like Robert Frost's poem, 'on its own melting'. The allowed and hallowed military discourse begins, but immediately finds its survival difficult: the initial momentum rapidly falters and fades away.

This structure of development and dissolution runs through the opening account of the Battle of the Wilderness, where the movement of the troops becomes the movement of the text towards the statuesque and the stabilized:

> The Union assault funneled itself right into a vision of sculptured artillery fire, and the Union troops suddenly found pieces of flying marble breaking their center and breaking their edges. At the instant of contact, history transformed their bodies into statues. They didn't like it, and the assault began to back up along the Orange Plank Road. What a nice name for a road. (*CG*, p. 18)

The known results of the war forbid its use as a story-line, unless one concerns oneself with the potential military associations and thematic diversions that chance to arise during the narration; the future – for Appomatox 'waits less than a year away' – confines the advancing line of the discourse. All movement is condemned to go the way the cowboys did when they were captured by Frederick Remington's chisel, or the Civil War troops did under the camera of Matthew Brady: into fixity. Historical discourse thus arrests imaginative action, leaving the mind free to concentrate only on irrelevant details. And the real text of the book will mould itself around these discursive lacunae and asperities, smuggling itself in trivial disguises into the margins of the official narrative. Thus, for example, the eye and the imagination are arrested and diverted by the name of the road on which the action takes place, the strange appearance of the Digger Indians, or their feeding of limpets to General Lee's horse, Traveller, the first horse they have seen – details none of which pertain to the main line of action the chapter half-heartedly offers to report. Meanwhile, immobility and inactivity respectively characterize the army as a whole and its Digger Indian members: every step entails retreat, funnels promise closures and dead ends, statues arrest all dynamics, ineluctability spells narrative entropy. The progression of things towards their known end can only signal their unmaking – the aborting of their original imaginative conception. The official theme moves towards its own collapse; meanwhile narrative culs-de-sac, which are the only thing left on the original programme, lay down a metaphorical network that the text will doggedly develop to produce its own perpetuation and coherence, an associative proliferation that will finally grow to give this satirical book 186,000 endings per second.

Straightforward narratives, then, can apparently give no hint of poetic truth; that is secreted in the cracks and crevices in the narrative. Once the reality of a Confederacy has been dissolved, Confederate generals cannot mean anything real. The true Augustus Mellon cannot be found, but in any case reality is not in books. For Jesse (the narrator), reading Ecclesiastes is rather like looking for the secrets of engineering (he counts the punctuation signs), while Lee Mellon prefers to 'read the frogs' that populate the pond of his Big Sur residence. The words that matter can only be those that refer to the present state of experience; hence Lee Mellon, born into fiction, has to start living 'in ruins' (*CG*, p. 20), and it is he who becomes 'the battle flags and drums of this book', that which makes the text march on despite all narrative obstacles. The rulings of history make it impossible for a Confederate general, fighting for an eliminated cause, to be anything more than an idea, an idea of resistance and gallantry; Lee, offered as the inheritor of those who once invented the radical American fiction of a new and independent state, can thus be only an absolute outsider, whose imaginative qualities none the less lend a propulsive power to the text. His great possession is 'a wonderful sense of distortion'; his imaginary origins grant him the disruptive force that permits him and the book to transgress the codes and regulations of 'military narrative'. Hence the book that starts is not the book that finishes; the 'book' referred to on page 20 is not the 'book' mentioned on page 160, for Lee (Robert E.) belongs in one type of book, Lee (Mellon), that 'Lee-of-another-color' (*CG*, p. 20), in another – or in none at all, since the one he lives in refuses to close, like the half-parentheses that recur in Brautigan's novels and poems.

Yet all the fantasies generated by the original notion of 'military narrative' hang from a borrowed structure: the military theme gathers all imaginative drifting around its lexical stronghold, in order to check aberrant developments. The pre-text thus does give its order to a text which, left to its own devices, could well have no limits. Hence, as the text grows more delirious, and ostensibly free from its origins, the story of Augustus Mellon intervenes ever more insistently; fictitious even in the fiction, he none the less gives the novel its 'red badge of homogeneity'. The military discourse continues to assert its presence, through a growing intrusion of episodes drawn from the old general's life, told in the manner of Stephen Crane's *The Red Badge of Courage*. For the modern characters, living in the fictional present, the discourse inherited from the past serves as a device of stabilization; but firm narrative orders are meanwhile constantly being overturned, by anachronism, non sequitur, mixed genres, free associations, unstable signifiers. Bedlam reigns, as the logic of the images threatens all narrative logics; in the anarchic world of Lee and Jesse, the precision of arbitrary figures (425 generals, 175 teeth, 163 cable cars, the 7452nd frog) acts both as a source of humour and as an ironic wink at the discourse of historical accuracy.

In *A Confederate General from Big Sur* a text lives out its freedom. However discontinuous the narrative thread may become, however unmotivated this allusion or that relationship, from one word or incident to the next, 'in its own way it makes sense' (*CG*, p. 95). Brautigan fights to preserve the independence of the text from the constraints of conventional narrative discourse; the 'battle' the text offers us is not the one we have been led to expect. Even as the military tale asserts itself more and more obtrusively, the text fights back by denouncing the vanity and oppressive structure of such narratives. Towards the book's end, Augustus Mellon is diverted elsewhere ('WHERE'S AUGUSTUS MELLON? *On the front page of the* Wilderness Bugle. *Turn to page 19 for Robert E. Lee. Turn to page 103 for an interesting story about alligators*'; *CG*, p. 129), and the reader is sent to circle back through the text; later Augustus Mellon is described as being entrapped in the codes of military behaviour and 'unable to cope with reality' (*CG*, p. 143). From then on, the text detaches itself increasingly from all and any reference. Images acquire a mounting arbitrariness, and the unity of bugles, headquarters, flanks, banners, sieges, marches and charges disappears: 'Elaine stared at the waves that were breaking like ice cube trays out of a monk's tooth or something like that. Who knows? I don't know' (*CG*, p. 154). A series of lightning flashes perpetuates rather than ends the book, which therefore achieves total freedom from the 'funnel-like' pressure of historical narratives, which fuse many elements into one unidirectional pattern and work towards one statuesque ending. The cone has been reversed, and this narrative explodes whatever laborious unity it had been pursuing, multiplying an abundance of unbounded, multidirectional futures, 'endings going faster and faster, more and more endings, faster and faster until this book is having 186,000 endings per second.' Endings thus follow the rules of possibilities and disintegrate with the speed of light. The necessary recycling of a ten-cent pomegranate, which had been accidentally introduced into the narrative machine several pages before this half-apocalyptic and half-epiphanic conclusion, testifies to the range of obligations and freedoms writing has to deal with. Illumination is a product of the battle fought by the text against narrative constraint, an act of 'magic lanterns with an endless waterfall of visions' (*Rommel*, p. 9).

*

As we shall see, the beginnings and endings of Brautigan's first three novels – or 'writings', as he used to call them – are all problematic, for structurally they express the fundamental duality of the act of representation in writing: the act which exhausts, encloses, defuses, cages and silences the magic of the creative moment, but which at the same time can make for an unlimited and unbounded freedom. All three of these first novels severally assert his rejection of everything static and fixed. The ideal target, in this respect, is the statue. *A Confederate General* began with statues – statistical as well as lapidary – and ended with the breaking of waves. *Trout Fishing in America* is likewise enacted between statues and waterfalls. It commences with a cover that depicts the author and a female companion standing in front of the statue of Benjamin Franklin, in San Francisco's Washington Square; it ends with the author planting in the text an unattached word he has always wanted to write. The book's epigraph forcefully dramatizes and mourns the simultaneous desirability and impossibility of preserving the most living of things for centuries of contemplation: 'There are seductions that should be in the Smithsonian Institute, right next to *The Spirit of St Louis*.' This is an apt introduction to a book which – by seeking to create 'the spirit of Trout Fishing in America' – attempts its own complex verbal seductions; and the pages we are about to open constitute a kind of museum, entered through the columns of the table of contents. The fluidity of *Trout Fishing in America* will be in constant opposition and counterpoint to the fixity reflected on the cover of the book.

That cover becomes the subject of the book's first chapter-essay, 'The Cover for Trout Fishing in America'. For the cover is a photograph, a still, a snapshot arresting reality, trapping it into a moment, a state of being (just as the prologue of *A Confederate General* presented us with an arrested, slowly disintegrating battlefield situation): on it, a man from the past and a man imprisoned in an already departed present are portrayed. Franklin's position and message alike spell out a condition of attrition: his life and live words have been superseded by 'a pedestal that looks like a house containing stone furniture', and, when 'the statue speaks', it delivers 'in marble' a message from its donor, H. D. Cogswell, which is poorly related to Poor Richard's poor aphorisms.[5] It is late afternoon on the 'cover for Trout Fishing in America': the poplars are almost leafless, the weather is dull, the cypress is 'almost dark like a room'. Closure, confinement and fixity are the message of the covers of all books, which lock in living speech; the disabling, sterilizing power of all such attempts to transcribe the real is epitomized in the banal inscription on the statue's pedestal, and the dislocated fragment from Dante's *Paradiso* ('Per L'Universo') over the church door ('La gloria di celui che tutto muove per l'universo penetra e risplende', reads the full phrase in Canto I – and on the actual monument). Brautigan also stands in the 'cover for Trout Fishing in America', and we are invited to see that his own subsequent enunciation will be similarly congealed.

Meanwhile, the tantalizing polysemy of the emphasized words 'cover for' promotes further ambiguities. The 'America' of the title borrows its official representation from established discourse and recognized myths (the irony of American promises is already seen in the crowds of the poor who gather to rush into the church for meagre spinach sandwiches); the book will

28

endeavour to redefine it. Likewise the protean 'hero' of the text will borrow his various utterances from the person who 'covers' and records his multifarious activities. When, later, we 'return to the cover of this book' on page 76, we find a letter from 'Trout Fishing in America', signed, however, in Brautigan's own handwriting; and his sleeping with 'a wet sheet wrapped around myself, to keep cool', feeling 'like a mental patient', returns us to those images of freezing and entrapment that serve as cover-metaphor for the whole of the text they encase. This is especially so because a link is established between that initial vision of the statue on the cover and the image of an enshrouded, insane person.

The section called 'The Shipping of Trout Fishing in America Shorty to Nelson Algren' offers to send Shorty, the 'legless, screaming middle-aged wino' who is the present representative of the American Dream, to the museum of Nelson Algren, a writer particularly known for his loving description of realistic detail and for naturalistic fascination with such characters. But instead Shorty is returned back to the cover of the book. We see him sitting in a laudromat in his wheelchair 'with closed eyes staring out of the window', a tranquil expression on his face: 'He almost looked human. He had probably fallen asleep while he was having his brains washed in one of the machines.' Wet sheet and mental patient are not far away: 'They probably swept him up one morning and put him in jail to punish him, the evil fart, or they put him in a nuthouse to dry him out a little', says the text, but then offers a better idea:

Trout Fishing in America Shorty should be buried right beside the Benjamin Franklin *statue* in Washington Square. We should *anchor* his wheelchair to a huge gray *stone* and *write upon the stone*:
> Trout Fishing in America Shorty
> 20c Wash
> 10c Dry
> Forever   (*TFA*, p. 47; my italics)

Not only are the allusions to 'brainwashing' here made crucial

29

to the book; also central is the link established between the statue-like handicapped figure in his wheelchair and the monumental founding father on the cover. Franklin's statue spells 'WELCOME' on all four sides; but the value of this 'optimistic' vision is everywhere challenged, not just by the world of the book but by the alternative inscription proposed here for Shorty's pedestal. Historical icons and discursive monuments therefore invite debunking; hence the insidious proposal in the passages quoted above that Franklin himself might be just another 'evil fart', and that all inscriptions on monuments, all marble forms, have exactly the same amount of relevance to reality as the prosaic, trivial epitaph proposed for Shorty.

*

Marble and statues are everywhere in Brautigan's work, from the earliest writings in *Revenge of the Lawn* (1971) to the latest, *The Tokyo–Montana Express* (1980). 'His voice is remembered down trails of sound colored hunting marble', reads one of 'The Lost Chapters of *Trout Fishing in America*' called 'Rembrandt Creek' in *Revenge of the Lawn*; elsewhere, simple events repeat themselves over and over again like a 'pale marble movie' (*RL*, p. 98). 'Lost cities' and endless 'shadows' bear testimony to immobilized things: the San Francisco Hall of Justice is a 'huge, tomb-like gloomy looking building and inside it always smells like rotten marble' (*DB*, p. 17). Marble is the tomb of language: 'Always at the end of the words somebody is dead' (*RL*, p. 169; though the context of this sentence is the narrator's attempt at announcing to his wife her father's death as best he can). The Confederate general is made a monument on the first attack; Benjamin Franklin's statue presides over a necessarily fossilized narrative; all the narrator of *In Watermelon Sugar* (1968) can do to assert his wish for fluidity and open-endedness is to sigh 'I had never had much luck at statues' (*IWS*, p. 75). Throughout Brautigan's work, statues constitute one facet of the rich iconography pointing to immobility and fixity. Everywhere, doors, rooms, cabins, out-

30

houses and shacks, girded spaces and enclosures, and solidities, fossilizations and opacities, are presented as victories for alienating and killing forms, so many small deaths of the poetic instance. Real death – that represented by corpses, tombs, coffins and cemeteries – is, of course, also present; but it is only one form of this larger death felt everywhere. For whatever does not move any longer – whatever is consumed, past, over, set for all time – provokes Brautigan's fear of the monumental and the eternally fixed; to Brautigan all should be motion, magic, life.

The watermelon sugar that constitutes the basic material of the world of iDEATH in *In Watermelon Sugar* is living light. Brautigan's characters are penetrated by the mellow light of days, the sweetness of words and things; Lee Mellon is the quicksilver denial of his marble ancestor. Life is limpid, quiet, perpetually flowing, and from this spring come the innumerable presences of water in his works. Trout creeks are absolute motion: 'water', 'melon', 'trout', 'Lee Mellon', 'trout fishing', 'watermelon sugar' – all stand for whatever shifts, sparkles, glows, illuminates and radiates. These contrasts are not simply the thematic base of Brautigan's works; they are the terms of a dialectical opposition between motion and immobility which provides his early texts with their fundamental tension, and pushes the reader beyond the referential towards a metafictional reading of the structure of his complex texts. For, if all words lead to death, if language cannot transcribe fluidity without itself becoming immediately fossilized and ossified, then why write? Why fix and immobilize anything, on any page?

Brautigan's very utterance seems to lie in the conducting of this interrogation. On the one hand, he feels a compulsive fascination for the written – or rather for that being written, for writing as act[6] – and a hope that anything written might just succeed in perpetuating the moment; on the other hand, he feels a fascinated repulsion, because at the same moment writing is killing. The result is a very active polarity which is far more than the classic 'life and death' preoccupation of so much writing. Here it is a tension between writing as life and the written object as cemetery, corpse or grave. 'The bookstore was a parking lot for used graveyards,' notes *Trout Fishing in America*. 'Thousands of graveyards were parked in rows like cars' (*TFA*, p. 22). The library in *The Abortion* (1971) is a morgue for defunct writings, the place where what Brautigan in another place calls 'the paper shadows of America' (*RL*, p. 120) can be found. These are the ghosts which in *A Confederate General* then come back to haunt the living: 'The cats darted into the brush like books into a library. It would take them a little while but hunger would return them to us like the classics: *Hamlet, Winesburg, Ohio*' (*CG*, p. 98). In this way, all writing, for Brautigan, is 'haunted'. Death may creep everywhere into lives ('the beautiful darkness of lives' is couched in the dead writing of the library in *The Abortion*); likewise there is of necessity a stock of dead words in language, of defunct formulae in literature. Hence past writing becomes an intertext, while in *In Watermelon Sugar* the entire American historical and literary pre-text is located in the dubious world of 'the Forgotten Works'.

This undercutting of pre-texts and intertexts is indeed part of a much more general attack, an assault on all fixed representational forms, from myths and codes to moral messages and ideological assertions. In *Trout Fishing in America*, Brautigan contrasts his longing for an authentic (if problematic) pastoral vision with the multiple expressions of a corrupted, modern pseudo-tradition, thus denouncing the destruction of the country's soul and its recuperation by the hypocritical messages of a commercialized, falsified present. He satirizes the incantations and images inherited from the American past, using codes and references from former times in order to deride present dubious political mythologies; the satirical approach to the lore of the American Dream thus destabilizes all the discourses that might seek to transcribe it. Literary representations of myths interlock with parody or pastiche of them; however, it is not so much the content of those messages that is put in question as the nature of the discourses that convey it. As fixed, obligatory points of passage for evoking an elusive, ever-changing reality,

they are represented as impoverishing blockages. When Brautigan pastiches the Stephen Crane version of the Civil War in *A
Confederate General*, or traditional versions of a riot in *Sombrero Fallout* (1976), it is not so much war and violence that are
being denounced as the naturalistic or the patriotic discourse
that 'explains' them. When Moby-Dick, having forsaken
Ahab, works for Jimmy Hoffa in 'The Symbol' (*Pill*, p. 195), it
is not Melville who is denounced; the aim is to free the myth
itself from the decayed forms in which it is wrapped.

Brautigan's allusions and parodies are not merely simplistic
attacks on past authors, their works, or the events they relate or
describe. His aim is to liberate their texts from the tradition in
which they have been locked, the public uses to which they
have been put, their enforced role in the national ideology.
Longfellow's 'hearing aid' and 'Evangeline's vagina' are re-
leased from their statutory duty, so that we can no longer pay
homage simply by recalling the poet's great age or the sex of his
heroine; Hemingway's death as announced on the cover of *Life*
magazine is similarly divorced from the hackneyed 'nada' the
media have associated with it. The obligatory mention of
Henry Miller in the Big Sur context ('Not that [Jesse] had
anything against Henry Miller'; *CG*, p. 196) must be corrected
by the indifference of Jesse's girlfriend to the mention of the
name. Walt Whitman is naturally enrolled to put some Gettys-
burg back into the new Civil War (*CG*, p. 94), but forty pages
later he is comically converted into a Smokey Bear fireman, and
Smokey Bear has already been associated with 'leukemia';
neither myth is allowed to grow stable in the anarchy of the
narrative. Brautigan foregrounds the literary origins of his
images and allusions all the better to debunk the role their
original creators have taken up in popular discourse when the
images collapse and the allusions are mocked and amended.
Such allusions are brought into a new system of reference, used
as foils and as indicators of the arbitrariness of all 'literary'
references ('The old woman had a little hotplate in her room.
She did all her "cooking" in there and never used the community kitchen. . . . There is a poem by Jules Laforgue about the

Luxemburg Gardens. The old woman's hotplate was not that poem'; *CG*, p. 40). The effect resembles Donald Barthelme's use of cultural chatter and newspaper *Dreck* in his writings, and likewise destabilizes the authority of all such references. A mere moustache can trigger a comparison between a shepherd and a 'young, skinny Adolph Hitler but friendly' (*TFA*, p. 34); since only the most elementary surfaces of the referent are brought into play, the deeper associations of the name lie shattered. In *Trout Fishing in America*, Byron, Frank Norris, Lewis Carroll, Kafka and many others are similarly put to the most trivial use in order to defuse their potential influence. On the other hand, however, surreptitious pastiches, unavowed borrowings and quotations (from Thoreau, Melville, Wordsworth) establish a deeper level beneath the surface. Even more muted literary and cultural allusions (standing on the edge of the western world; going to sleep for a long time; crossing the continent, etc.), having had their official or their clichéd associations stripped away, can then be evoked for innovative re-use.

But, for all this denunciation of the obstructive presence of past writing and writers, Brautigan never forgets that he is expected to act as a writer too. Numerous allusions to his official function are strewn through his works. 'You're supposed to be literary,' the narrator is told in *A Confederate General* (*CG*, p. 152), a book in which the names of at least twenty-five other writers are dropped. The debris of ancient or previous writings always encumbers their successors, and his books are frequently embarrassed by their author's previous work (this is a key theme of *The Abortion*). Everywhere the remains of past texts are evoked and derided, through pastiche, parody or pun. The complex jigsaw puzzle extends even beyond the literary; Brautigan's creation, Trout Fishing in America Shorty, is handed on to the cinema in a film entitled 'Trout Fishing in America Shorty, Mon Amour'. Used forms are everywhere, and, while they congeal ideology, fix codes and preserve established referential systems, they none the less demand incorporation into any new text. Brautigan's humorous hijackings are both a denunciation and a recuperation. How can one write, he seems to exclaim on every page, when the history of discourse and literature invades one's own linguistic endeavours, intruding cliché, *déjà-vu*, the 'static lines' and 'paper shadows of America', recycling materials that block one's creative horizons quite as effectively as stone walls and other physical obstacles?

Writing that cannot establish its distance from already colonized linguistic territory condemns itself to a kind of death. Hence the themes of mutation, transformation and loosening, which are, as Brautigan sees it, at life's centre, can develop only through escape from whatever might mummify them. There must be some isomorphic relationship between doing, being and saying; perpetual change, shifts and slidings in experience, must be expressed through constant metamorphoses, transitions and fractures in the writing itself. As Jack Hicks once noted, 'a broad strain in recent fiction denies fixed styles and forms, as if "closed" modes (short story, novel, sustained discourse) were rigid cultural projections of a totalitarian mind.'[7]

※

These themes develop further in *In Watermelon Sugar* (1968), an idiosyncratic chronicle of life in the semi-utopian community of iDEATH. The graphic descriptions of threatening closure that open the two previous books are here replaced by strategic syntactical moves which appear like an abstract speculation on the methods of those earlier novels. For, in spite of Brautigan's sense that a few possibilities do exist for combating the programmatic closure of all creative writing, he seems fully conscious of the difficulties to be overcome. His resulting strategy seems to work at two levels: on the one hand, he strives to show how conscious he is of the artifices at work, while, on the other, he manages to avoid the traps they set, reopening texts that are moving towards their own closure. His method may be said to resemble a double demonstration *ad absurdum*. In *In Watermelon Sugar* one might thus first notice a central

35

notion: all reality is mobile, unsteady, fluctuating, and life is not a continuum but an accretion of moments, transitory and ephemeral states. From this follows the constant powerful questioning of the very notion of identity, which is perpetually destroyed and renewed. The question even applies to the narrator, and the chapter 'My Name' is particularly significant in this respect. Ishmael is out-Ishmaeled: 'I am one of those who do not have a regular name. My name depends on you. Just call me whatever is in your mind.' The narrator's name becomes a proliferating list of possibilities:

> If you are thinking about something that happened a long time ago: Somebody asked you a question and you did not know the answer.
> That is my name.
> Perhaps it was raining very hard.
> That is my name. . . . (*IWS*, pp. 4–5)

This can figure as a commentary on Brautigan's constant play with signifiers and signifieds, signs and referents; but it is also an illustration of the principles that govern in the world of iDEATH, in which the book is set.

Hence the sense of fundamental lexical difference in this work. 'Trout Fishing in America' changed from being a title to a signifier with multiple signifieds – in turn hotel, place, person, nickname, adjective, author, nature, narrator, book and sport. Its centre was everywhere but its precise circumference was nowhere, allowing a semantic dissemination. However, in *In Watermelon Sugar*, nothing enables the reader to specify the reality of things, or even to name them. This time the inquiry takes place not in polysemy but in anomie or anonymity; the language uses whatever is vague, fuzzy, ill defined, blurred, moving, shifting. Most words in the book are indefinite and boundless, and thus foreground the syntactical structure at the expense of lexical precision:

> Margaret started poking around for *things* that she might *like*. . . .
> I sat down on *something* that *looked like* a wheel and

watched Margaret take a forgotten *sticklike thing* and poke
around a small pile of stuffed *things*.

I saw *something* lying at my feet. . . .

'Have you found *anything* you *like*?' I said. (*IWS*, p. 71;
my italics)

The introverted structure confers on to all sentiments ('to like')
the evanescence of an arbitrary comparison ('like'), and this
echoes the vagueness of pervasive feelings which stands for
social structure in iDEATH. In fact, society itself becomes
paratactic, an accumulation of mere individual elements with
no clear subordinative pattern – a way of writing, incidentally,
that is characteristic of much contemporary fiction. The death
of identity – symbolized in the word 'iDEATH' itself – is
extended to the whole environment. Indeed, all definitions here
are caused by the environment, which is hence linguistic; one is
reminded of Saussure's definition of language as a system the
components of which have meaning only in so far as they are
part of that system. Successive infiltrations and osmoses define
change by illustrating it: 'iDEATH is always changing'. It is 'the
indescribable way it changes that we like so much, that suits us'
(*IWS*, p. 62). The recurrence of such 'suits us' and 'suits me' in
the text implies the eminent plasticity of the self, which adapts
to whatever state that iDEATH assumes.

iDEATH may well be the death of the ego; it is also that of
fixed ideas, and of the words we use to designate them. So, just
as in *Trout Fishing in America* signifiers are traded as in some
game of semantic musical chairs, and so lose their substance in
reality, here we live among substanceless substances:

Fred had something strange-looking sticking out of the
pocket of his overalls. I was curious about it. It looked like
something I had never seen before.

'What's that in your pocket, Fred?'

'I found it today coming through the woods up from the
Watermelon Works. I don't know what it is myself. I've
never seen anything like it before. What do you think it is?'

He took it out of his pocket and handed it to me. I didn't

know how to hold it. I tried to hold it like you would hold a flower and a rock at the same time.

'How do you hold it?' I said.

'I don't know. I don't know anything about it.' (*IWS*, pp. 6–7)

For Brautigan, 'man's desire to name the objects of the world' is the cross and Golgotha of his imagination (*Pill*, p. 5). Refusing that desire, he opts for the utmost arbitrariness of signs. His open questioning of stable signifieds, his constant recourse to what might be called 'travelling signifiers', is a first breach in the fixity of literary forms, an immediate utterance of his suspicion of discourse, an expression of the preference he gives to what Roman Jakobson calls the poeticity of the text. Since a fluctuating environment produces ever-renewed and different realities, any search for isomorphic expression must admit the abolition of stabilized signs. Though the narrator is writing a book, no book has been written for thirty-five years in iDEATH, and only twenty-three over the last 171 years; existing books have been burned to take advantage of the warmth they could thereby provide. The local newspaper comes out only once a year, probably when iDEATH 'is in one of its many and lasting forms', an oxymoronic formulation which expresses the impossibility of anything *written* and anything *new* coexisting.

This is revealed in the conflict between inBOIL and iDEATH, where inBOIL preserves codified knowledge, violence, perpetual reference, and iDEATH, with its trout hatchery built on the ashes of tigers, preserves the elusive graceful spontaneity of fish. Yet even here there is the inevitable possibility of closure. 'What's [your book] about?' Doc Edwards asks the narrator. 'Just what I'm writing down,' he answers: 'one word after another' (*IWS*, p. 107). But the narrator's ex-teacher, who commends his star pupil's work, has not left the world of traditional criticism ('Your description of the winter clouds was very accurate and quite moving at the same time and contained a certain amount of poetic content. Yes, I am quite interested in reading your book'; *IWS*, pp. 44–5). Even though play is the main activity in this city of words, Brautigan syntactically spells out the inevitable circularity of speech: 'In watermelon sugar the deeds were done and done again as my life is done in watermelon sugar,' the book begins. The idea of 'travel', which immediately follows on, suggests the uncertain hope of making it safely to the other end of the text with minimal equipment, the only justification for the attempt being a sort of communication partially devoid of message:

> I'll tell you about it because I am here and you are distant.
> Wherever you are, we must do the best we can. It is so far to travel, and we have nothing here to travel, except watermelon sugar. I hope this works out. (*IWS*, p. 1)

Book One ends on the words 'I thought', Book Two on 'I dreamt', Book Three on 'I wrote'. The words, placed as they are, can either represent the usual deictic device used in writing to locate the source of speech or information, or act as a metafictional gesture by which the reader's attention is drawn to imagining, dreaming, and writing itself.

The concluding 'I wrote' particularly stands out. A dance is about to begin; the musicians get ready; the lights are on; the trout are swimming; the narrator has not mentioned his writing for pages. Then comes the last paragraph: 'The musicians were poised with their instruments. They were ready to go. It would only be a few seconds now, I wrote' (*IWS*, p. 138). Just when the end is in sight, when the circle of the text is about to be completed, the reader is thrown back to a-referentiality by a direct and brutal allusion to the written nature of the book. One of the most descriptive sections of the work aborts its claim to suspension of disbelief by restricting the referential subject to the veracity of the writer's act. Curiously, the book then ends with an *hors-texte* note which describes the dates and places of the book's writing, and calls it a 'novel'. Thus the narrator is literally *extracted* from his story at the last minute, his final words prying him away from the deadly circularity of the first, rather like a test-pilot ejected from his crashing plane on what would have been his last flight.

3

THE DRIFTWOOD ARTIST

Language does not leave fossils, at least not until it has become written. *(Trout Fishing in America)*

The world as literary object eludes us; knowledge deserts literature which can no longer be mimesis or mathesis [a structured field of knowledge] but only semiosis, adventure of the impossibilities of language. In a word, text. It is incorrect to say that the notion of a text reduplicates that of literature; literature represents a finite world, the text figurates the infinite in language, devoid of all knowledge, reason, intelligence. (Roland Barthes, *Barthes par lui-même* (1975))

Brautigan's rejection of fixed forms is the lasting concern of his three early novels, but there can be little doubt that the text which most clearly invites the reader to share in his literary reflexiveness is *Trout Fishing in America*. Denouncing the confinement enforced by discursive description of a complex reality – a reality that such discursive description cannot in fact contain, so that such writing becomes a fabricated ensemble, an ornamental artifice – this book attempts to generate an original mode of structure and imagery. As most of the critics have noted, the basic material of this, his best-known and probably his best 'novel', is a vision of the American West, an exploration of the relationship of the self to this classic field of pastoral, and a lament for the destruction of the American Dream by a trivial culture. As Manfred Pütz has demonstrated, this thematic orientation is also an aesthetic situation. Brautigan's native Pacific Northwest is thoroughly 'fished out' in *Trout Fishing*; indeed, amateurs of local colour can easily identify these landscapes and settings, which are also present in the poems of Gary Snyder, the novels of Tom Robbins, and Ken Kesey's *Sometimes a Great Notion*. 'Trout fishing', in the text, means an intimate contact with these regions, though they may be more a pretext than an actual topic. It is, of course, possible to draw conclusions by focusing on the explicit activities of the book's narrator: Brautigan observes that 'somehow the Long Tom River was a part of my spiritual DNA' (*RL*, p. 164), and one can find in the book an old theme, set somewhere between the writings of Thoreau on the one hand, and Sinclair Lewis's Nobel Prize address on the other – 'I learned as a boy, that there is something very important about catching fish, if you have no need of doing so.'

Yet this idea is also the object of Brautigan's demythologization. The few sections of the book devoted to real fishermen are cruelly and firmly negative, and the book subverts the entire 'All-American fish-and-game' establishment, reducing *Field and Stream* to the status of a scandal sheet. However, one might argue that, though there are no more trout in *Trout Fishing* than bears (or Vietnams) in Norman Mailer's *Why are we in Vietnam?*, the book emphasizes not the success or failure of such expeditions but the nature of the quest. The book's development may be close to that of Hemingway's 'Big Two Hearted River', or *The Torrents of Spring*, but Hemingway is also rejected, for the lore of muscular achievement is alien here. Indeed, the achievement-oriented redneck fisherman is probably the dinosaur the trout elude in Brautigan's poetry:

> A trout-colored wind blows
> through my eyes, through my fingers
> And I remember how the trout
> used to hide from the dinosaurs . . .
> The trout hid in subways, castles
> and automobiles. They waited patiently
> for the dinosaurs to go away. (*Pill*, p. 35)

In the world of dinosaurs, the trout are threatened; the oppositions new/old, live/fixed, free/fettered which run through all these first three novels are active here. Yet none of this gives us a sufficient reading; there is no way of following the motif and myth called up by the title as a guiding principle from start to

41

finish. The pastoral theme and the myths, even if demythologized, do not provide us with the stuff of a 'unified' and 'homogeneous' reading. Another guide is needed if we are to give the 'bookness' back to the book, and this guide is the writing itself.

For the confessed ramblings and wanderings of the narrator in this work are strictly artificial, and the real 'picaresque' here is verbal: 'traveling along the good names' (*TFA*, p. 78). The only itinerary the reader can follow is one that uses the map of stylistic phenomena. Recourse to the referent does not provide an analysis; little advantage is gained from comparing the literary experience with 'reality'. Since most parts of the text are polysemic, a plural reading is the only way to unify it. Not only do the signifiers take over from the thematics; they provide the only propelling element in a book that is otherwise simply anecdotal. Yet *Trout Fishing* is *not* a collection of short stories either, for the interplay of signifiers in their harmonic development gives the book its strongest structural reality. In the fifth chapter, a drunk creates 'his own Kool-Aid reality and was able to illuminate himself by it' (*TFA*, p. 10); the text does the same. Trout and reader progress by jumping after artificial flies, and the unity of the progression relies fundamentally on the possible logics arising from the image. Certainly there is a central stock of images that are referential: trout, fishing, America. And at the referential level they call up those elements already referred to: the realm of fishing, nature, equipment, animals, pastoral, seasons, sensory correspondences. They also open on to an alternative stock, where violence and aggression replace peace and quiet, impurity replaces purity, technological disruption invades ecological harmony. From the opening pages, where two contending worlds compete for the same image (Andrew Carnegie, trout-fishing for steel, and the 'people with three-cornered hats fishing in the dawn'; *TFA*, p. 3), the essential oscillation begins – between the bucolic, mythical America of colonial times, and a modern world far removed from them. So snow, creek, dew, sugar and music are set against death, autumn, graveyards, cypresses and sheep;

these images of peace are in turn pitted against figures of living death through violence (Billy the Kid, Dillinger), aggressive instruments of destruction of the natural life (camping craze, surgeon, winos, urban depradation) and images of lethal immobility (doors, houses, mirrors, statues).

The conflict and co-operation of these 'static' images also, however, go on to give birth to another set of what we might call 'autonomous' images – mostly bizarre, unexpected similes and metaphors which clash with the backdrop of references to standard genres and draw together disparate elements, as if to escape from the logic of the original oppositions (pastoral/urban, etc.). Often they do not generate text beyond their own length: thus 'His eyes were like the shoelaces of a harpsichord' (*TFA*, p. 26); 'It was very much like the sound of an insect laying the 1,000,000th egg of our disaster' (*TFA*, p. 39); 'The sun was like a huge fifty-cent piece that someone had poured kerosene on and then had lit with a match and said, "Here, hold this while I go get a newspaper," and put the coin in my hand, but never came back' (*TFA*, p. 6). Never taken up again, they simply wrench the reader's attention away from the apparent subject and destabilize the system of reference. They are iconographic witticisms disrupting the referential base, but they do not block the discursive flow. Brautigan can then, indeed, comment ironically on the failure of his images to take off from the text and carry it along with them. In *A Confederate General* the method is more explicit, and openly points to the signifier-activated propulsion of the text: 'The wind made me think about the battle of Agincourt for it moved like arrows about us, through the very air. Ah, Agincourt, the beauty is all in the saying' (*CG*, p. 112). More complex is the motif of the alligators, whose 'Growl! – opp-opp-opp-opp-opp-opp-opp-opp' is silenced when Lee uses one to eat his dinner on, for 'tables should not say things like that' (*CG*, p. 112). Sometimes the imaginative flight leads only to an early landing, generating no sizeable consequences; elsewhere referential reality refuses to melt, for the sake of coherence, under imaginative pressure, as in the closing lines of the third section of

Trout Fishing in America: '"Excuse me," I said. "I thought you were a trout stream." "I'm not," she said' (*TFA*, p. 5). Here a stubborn, unimaginative reality denies the suspension of disbelief the image has proposed, as compared with the opposite effect in *A Confederate General*: 'Lee Mellon . . . tapped his head with his finger in the fashion people do to see if a watermelon is ripe. It was' (*CG*, p. 73).

But, in the best cases, Brautigan's images can 'take hold' and 'catch on', become part of the very dynamic of the narrative itself, so enfranchising his text from discursive necessities and generating free creation on the narrative margins. While in the examples above the 'autonomous' embryos of poetic text lack the momentum to break free of the narrative logic, and while the 'rebel' images of *A Confederate General* can never quite displace the 'military narrative', there are times when a string of dynamic images will achieve victory. In one attempt in *Trout Fishing in America*, Brautigan offers us (1) 'a row of old houses, huddled together like seals on a rock' (*TFA*, p. 4), merely static images from the Pacific west coast referential stock; (2) 'At a distance I saw a waterfall come pouring down off the hill', a similar referential item; and (3) 'I walked home past the glass whiskers of the houses, reflecting the downward rushing waterfalls of night.' The passage from simile to metaphor displays the image taking off from mere thematic reference, as the seals of (1) lend their whiskers to the houses of (3). However, the 'waterfalls' of (3), by reinstating the reference of (2), return us to the level of thematic discourse, and the attempt stops short. None the less the verbal rather than the referential plot is the one that eventually comes to structure *Trout Fishing in America*, generating linkages from sentence to sentence, paragraph to paragraph, section to section, and so providing what unity and organization the book has. This is why, to grasp the book, we need to explore what Tolstoy called the 'labyrinth of linkages' – and why we need to establish a 'poetic' or metafictional reading.

*

Brautigan's methods of simple linkage from sentence to sentence can be displayed in the movement from simile to metaphor in the example of the grocer's red birthmark (*TFA*, p. 9). What starts as simile ('He was bald with a red birthmark on his head. The birthmark looked just like an old car parked on his head') develops into a shifting, generative device: 'He nodded and the old red car wobbled back and forth on the road as if the driver were having an epileptic seizure.' The simile-turned-metaphor allows a new simile to be created, thus extending its narrative potential. But there are more complex generative patterns, giving birth to entire paragraphs and sections. The ninth section of the book, 'The Ballet for Trout Fishing in America', takes its coherence from a dynamic of images remote from the ostensible drive of the book. Brautigan says that 'The main energy for the ballet comes from a description of the Cobra Lily' – and this is established by a complex network of combinations taking us from burial to hell, through can, graveyard, wreath and mortuaries, often by random association. The can in which the dead flower is buried lists the artificial ingredients of Metrecal; the 'natural' characteristics of the flower are provided in the form of encyclopedic data, then rendered distorted and absurd. All this must be converted into the ephemerality of ballet, by a miraculous holding together of components through motion: the dancers 'hold our imagination in their feet' (*TFA*, pp. 15–16). It is such leapings from image to image, or bait to bait, that provide the dynamic unity of a text that would otherwise consist of incompatible fragments.

Similar principles tie together whole sections of the book. Thus, in one section which does actually deal with *trout fishing*, in *America* – the section called 'The Hunchback Trout' – the organization derives from the elaboration and dislocation of iconographic clusters around absent signifieds. One hidden allusion is to Quasimodo, the Hunchback of Notre-Dame, developed through the good fellow/Jack the Ripper opposition, the association of white cat/fall from a high place, a hump, and finally the reference at the end, when the fish is eaten and

45

'its hump tasted sweet as the kisses of Esmeralda.' The drama of the catch is being translated into terms remote from fishing, just as the pastoral landscape is meantime being turned into an alien technical landscape: 'The creek was like 12,845 telephone booths in a row with high Victorian ceilings and all the doors taken off and all the backs of the booths knocked out.' Here even the item used as a comparison in the simile is utterly dismantled – but its linguistic presence lingers on, to be used throughout the section. The telephone image persists, allowing the angler to become a telephone repairman, permitting the size of the trout to be compared with long-distance calls, and the fishing line with a line for transmitting sound – so leading to a string of similes about the sound, and then the colour, of ambulances. That 'life energy' which the narrator feels 'screaming back up the line to my hand' as the fish feeds his line is experienced just when the digressions and similes seem to reach exhaustion; it leads on to the actual 'catch' and the author's tribute to the fish's energy, of which he then wants to make a 'death mask'. Secret metaphorical bridges have thus replaced the apparent task of providing a fishing description from an angler's notebook, and Brautigan seems to celebrate his own victory (his 'catch') over simple discursiveness. In addition, there is a continual semantic lag: the images constantly occur before the action they prepare the reader for. The hook always keeps falling slightly ahead of the fish (even though, in the end, life-energy mobility leads to death-mask fixity). Such stylistic leaps produce a sense of displacement and of creative discovery.

Such decentrings, occurring everywhere throughout the book, imply that reality can in the end lie only in the autonomous world of signs. A variety of systems of linkage – from simple repetition of references to, say, drama and cinema, to iconic and phonetic mating (such alliterative strings as sun, sheep, smell, shadows on page 50, for instance) – provide the basis of creative activity. The image web passes on from section to section; for instance, the end of one chapter provides matter the next one will use (the cobra lily of the 'Ballet' section prepares us for the flesh-eating plant which opens the following section, etc.). These extended systems of images thus cumulatively disrupt the discursive text, supporting the view that America is 'often only a place in the mind'; and when, as Jesse says, 'the mind takes a vacation from the senses' (*CG*, p. 153), when impressions, sensory correspondences and associative images replace referential transcription, each signifier grows thicker and more suggestive, making it what Mayakovsky calls a 'self-valuable word', a word so enriched in signification that its function is shifted from that of vehicle to that of agent. The cumulative process is finally a return to the book's theme, for the America of the title is now emptied of all reliable content. As André Breton put it in the surrealist manifestos, images become 'the only handlebars of the mind in a vertiginous race'. Gradually the text takes over, to such an extent that its poeticity replaces the initial argument as the main centre of interest. Language makes its official *raison d'être* irrelevant or obsolete. Like Chateaubriand hypothetically travelling in the Holy Land, we must, seizing our lexical Baedeker, travel 'along the good names'.

*

But there still remains in *Trout Fishing in America* a group of 'meta-images' that bring us closer still to Brautigan's method and which, pointing to the writing process itself, finally integrate the book. They appear mostly in the chapters the critics have found hardest to cope with, those that lie outside its obvious thematic or its direct symbolic logic, like 'The Mayonnaise Chapter' and its 'Prelude', 'Another Method of Making Walnut Catsup', 'A Half-Sunday Homage to a Whole Leonardo da Vinci' and 'Trout Fishing in America Nib'. Here occur certain essential motifs of 'mixtures', 'montage' and 'recipe', of 'appearance', 'decoration' and 'writing', which offer the prism through which a reading might be suggested. Brautigan's fear of the entrapping circularity of discourse is confirmed in the section called 'The Cleveland Wrecking Yard', where many of the most referential images of the book are brought together, but as spare parts in a wrecking yard. Insects, water, plants and animals — the components of the original pastoral — are gathered under a hangar, some covered with tarpaulins, as if they might be used again. Yet the montage Brautigan has organized to make the book is taken apart, broken up, disposed of, its parts being auctioned off at a low price. The loop is looped; now even the insects that have populated the book are locked up in boxes for sale. The image of the 'wrecking yard' is an image commenting on the use of images, a display of the way the previous 'mixtures' of the book have 'turned' or 'soured'. This passage, then, gives a perspective on the way in which the various 'recipes' of the book may be put to use.

Brautigan's 'recipes' may be based on foods and condiments ready for imaginative consumption; they may be founded on elements of hardware ingeniously reassembled to make a verbal 'lure' (*TFA*, p. 108); they may, like Kool-Aid, be concocted to serve each individual's own need for illumination. But it is the idea of something cooked up or fabricated that Brautigan pursues. From the false fir trees of 'Trout Fishing in America Nib' to the phoney spirits of 'The Kool-Aid Wino', through optical illusions ('Knock on Wood (Part Two)') and fictitious prescriptions, everything converges towards a denunciation of the prefabricated, including all ready-made literary cuisines. *Trout Fishing in America* comes out, in effect, as a kit, with a few sample models suggesting possible ways of assembling it; how to put together and then take apart various narrative systems is the book's 'message'. With the kit, going through the various steps of word, sentence, paragraph, chapter and book, everything is possible. As a bonus, a few automatic structures, clichés, routine discursive hinges and hackneyed rhymes are provided free: 'in the pines, in the pines where the sun never shines' (*TFA*, p. 15); 'I felt just like a telephone repairman, even though I did not look like one. . . . I was an asset to society' (*TFA*, p. 55). A certain circularity creeps in here. The section 'Room 208, Hotel Trout Fishing in America' is a wonderful funhouse that the author of *Lost in the Funhouse*, John Barth, could hardly repudiate; indeed, Barth was one of the first to point out that Brautigan's work was not as simple as it seemed.[8] One walks round and round into the chapter, following the cat whose name, among other things, the figure 208 actually is, sharing acts of imagination, fictions that are both purposeful and purposeless, participating in the composition, entering the author's kitchen.

As in all cuisine, everything is a matter of proportions and *tour de main*. There are ways of boiling an egg 'well', and the simplest is not necessarily the most primitive. These compositional images indicate that Brautigan is simultaneously aware of the predictability, contrivance and mere consumption involved in literary creation, and of the fact that there is always one new way of cooking things up, for a drop of this or that will turn a stale recipe into a new dish. This, perhaps, is why, looking at two possible images for creation, that of the artist and that of the engineer, he prefers the instrument of the pen-nib over the fish-hook.

> I saw [Leonardo] inventing a new spinning lure for trout fishing in America. I saw him first of all working with his imagination, then with metal and color and hooks, trying a little of this and a little of that, and then adding motion and then taking it away and then coming back again with a different motion, and in the end the lure was invented. (*TFA*, p. 108)

Here the narrator displays one method of making the reader bite. But in the end he prefers the more impressionable working of the pen:

> 'Write with this, but don't write hard because this pen has got a gold nib, and a gold nib is very impressionable. After a while it takes on the personality of the writer. Nobody else can write with it. This pen becomes just like a person's shadow. It's the only pen to have. But be careful.'
>
> I thought to myself what a lovely nib trout fishing in America would make with a stroke of cool green trees along

the river's shore, wild flowers and dark fins pressed against the paper. (*TFA*, p. 110)

There has been much discussion of the last, misspelled word of *Trout Fishing in America*: 'mayonaise'. 'Expressing a human need, I always wanted to write a book that ended with the word Mayonnaise,' Brautigan has just told us (*TFA*, p. 111); but it is important to see the context in which that 'need' is expressed. It occurs in the 'Prelude to the Mayonnaise Chapter', which is devoted to linguistic theories and includes a comment on the way language becomes fossilized when written. After this 'prelude' the book ends with a letter of condolence on the death of Mr Good, with its postscript: 'P.S. Sorry I forgot to give you the mayonaise.' The connection between this wilful misspelling and the culinary imagery that is strewn throughout the book should not be ignored; and the culminating arbitrary distortion must be judged against the background of stale discourse which the platitudinous final letter illustrates. A double measure of the arbitrary offers a last chance to save the text from its threatening discursive closure, now that all the expected ingredients have been variously mixed and stirred. The last word sums up the book's attempt to point beyond the text to possibilities of unconventional literary creativity, which the departures from regular syntax and the independent logic of the imagery have sought to achieve. Brautigan's images – most of them, as we have seen, starting from similes – seem to me to be the pre-eminent signs of a will to depart from the referential fabric and establish a new network of equivalences in the margins of narration. It is as if, at the end of each referential presentation, a concentrated lump of harmonic meaning was pushed to the borders of the discourse, where poetic rather than narrative or thematic meaning was born. The unity of the text, in this perspective, would not only be the result of the hinging together of images, but also that of a constant and progressive extraction, whose end-product was crystallized and processed on the edge of the writing. Since this resulting 'sugariness' is a distillation of the text, not merely a sauce to decorate it, it is its very essence, oozing out of the reality it circumscribes. Out of such distilled visionary matter Brautigan paints his America.

Which is why 'Trout Fishing in America', as a spirit and a vision, cannot be defined, as in the end it never is. Its centre is everywhere and its circumference nowhere definable: it penetrates the things out of which it is made. Most of this visionary feeling itself comes from images, takes refuge within them and is concentrated there. Often based on incompatible couplings (like 'the metal intestine' of the wing that is 'retractable and visionary', in *The Abortion*), they are not so much 'surreal' as 'para-real', in so far as they are not only born out of what they convey but also lie outside it and replace it on its periphery. In *Trout Fishing in America*, it is the germinal aspect of the images that seems most emphatic (the most famous early collection of Brautigan's poems was entitled *Please Plant This Book*); their flowering on the edges of the official argument is what gives the text its true nature. Basic and naïve pastoral is transcended and displaced –

> Once, while cleaning out the trout before I went home in the almost night, I had a vision of going over to the poor graveyard and gathering up grass and fruit jars and tin cans and markers and wilted flowers and bugs and weeds and clods and going home and putting a hook in the vise and tying a fly with all that stuff and then going outside and casting it up into the sky, watching it float over clouds and then into the evening star. (*TFA*, p. 21)

– but the desertion of nature by America is compensated by the germinative effect of images whose function goes beyond mere referentiality. Above the surface of the discursive text, the flowers and meadows of America then bloom anew. Ironically, the power of imagery, while it frees the text from enslavement to reference, reconstitutes the destroyed themes para-realistically in the margins.

In this manner, one may agree, Brautigan is indeed a 'marginal' writer.

4

LIBRARIES AND LABORATORIES:
A GALLERY OF MONSTERS

The right words found him. (*The Hawkline Monster*)

Poetry is but one of the destinies of speech. (Gaston Bachelard, *L'Intuition de l'instant*)

If, as Flaubert said, style is continuity, then even *The Abortion* (1971), the least convincing of Brautigan's work to date, can still offer us instructive information about the relationship of the author to his work. Brautigan's earlier books had concealed their ambiguity within the text. *The Abortion* immediately defines itself. It is subtitled 'An Historical Romance', and claims to be 'a novel about the romantic possibilities of a public library in California'. The apparent mixing of genres in the subtitle has a source: the book was written when abortion was illegal in the USA but appeared after its legalization; hence 'historical' was added to the subtitle. But the book indeed straddles several genres, and begins a stage in his work where 'genre wars' were to become a lasting preoccupation. It thus appropriately marks a new chapter both in Brautigan's writing and in this book.

The Abortion is a thin book, though the longest of Brautigan's first four, and its weighty didactic passages, its ponderous load of banal ideas, its acquiescence in traditional structure, linearity and discursiveness, make it almost 'un-Brautiganesque'. Yet, clearly, Brautigan's former preoccupations have not entirely disappeared from a book that is focused on a man's relationship to books. As early as *A Confederate General*, Jesse cannot avoid perusing the books on Elaine's shelves: 'She closed the door and I glanced at her books, a very bad habit of mine. Hello *Collected Poems* of Dylan Thomas' (*CG*, p. 91). Similarly, arriving in Tijuana, the special librarian of *The Abortion* 'Couldn't help but look at the books in the window. They were different from the books that we had in the library' (*A*, p. 150). Indeed, the library the narrator had spontaneously chosen to run a few years earlier, dropping all other activities, is of a special kind. Here, unique works are brought in by their authors in manuscript form, as soon as they are finished, so that they can be buried at random in a morgue-like San Francisco library until their 'Foster' parent (Foster is the character's name) carts them out to a northern California grave. Already their real life – being written – is over; and the 'gentle attention' the librarian gives these authors is all the attention these half-literary works will ever receive. One of the twenty-three received on the day the novel begins was written by a certain Richard Brautigan:

> The author was tall and blond and had a long yellow mustache that gave him an anachronistic appearance. He looked as if he would be more at home in another era.
>
> This was the *third or fourth* book he had brought to the library. Every time he brought in a new book he looked a little older, a little more tired. He looked quite young when he brought in his first book. I can't remember the title of it, but it seems to me the book had something to do with America.
>
> 'What's this one about?' I asked, because he looked as if he wanted me to ask him something.
>
> 'Just another book,' he said. (*A*, p. 28; my italics)

Thus in Brautigan's mind there is clearly no difference between the fate reserved for the special books that end up in this special library and the books he has written himself. The title of the mythical work is 'Moose'; it is mentioned in a section called 'Buffalo Gals, Won't You Come Out Tonight?' Doubtless the hesitation between 'third or fourth book' arises from the fact that, at this point, the 'fourth' is not quite finished; the reference thus doubles back towards the book we read. However, what matters here is the implication that all literary creation ends up in seclusion and a sort of death, and that Brautigan's own books have the same destiny as all 'the lyrical and haunted volumes of American writing' (*A*, p. 96). The writer-librarian, severed from life, is a producer of still-born objects – a matter that cannot be overlooked in a book called *The Abortion*. Unable, like the soldier in *A Confederate General*, 'to cope with reality', he finds his reactions to the outside world systematically couched in literary terms: 'I hadn't realized that being in that library for so many years was almost like being in some kind of timeless thing. Maybe an airplane of books, flying through the pages of eternity' (*A*, p. 75). And, when an actual flight occurs, the 'description' of it brings us back again to the primary reality of print: not only does the airport look like something out of a slick erotic magazine, but landscapes themselves become no more than a combination of signs ('Vida looked out the window at what is not worth describing, but even more so and done in cold cement freeway language'; *A*, p. 157). Elsewhere 'a big white garage' is described as having 'a big word in blue on [its] front: . . . GULF' (*A*, p. 35). Such effects, recurrent throughout the book, and the various allusions to Brautigan's own status as cult hero, suggest a wistful attempt to bridge the gap, not just between words and realities, but between a brilliant first part and a rather trivial plot, as distant from 'history' as it is from 'romance'. Not that bridging the gap makes this a better book; but it does allow us to see it as a transitional creation between the idiosyncratic poetic revolts of the first three books and the seemingly different series of books that follow, the novels devoted to what I will call the 'genre wars'. Encapsulated in this disturbingly uneven novel may well be Brautigan's meditation on the work he has done and the striking new work that lies ahead.

Indeed, the notion of 'abortion' which dominates the book may itself be an allusion to his previous works. Ideas of foetal and existential death and rebirth permeate the book. When the female character, Vida (Spanish for 'life'), takes the short trip to the airport in the 'egg-like' van – a trip that acts as a hinge between the narrator's life in the library and his move to Tijuana's 'Kingdom of Fire and Water', where Vida will have an abortion – this imagery is at its most complex. Meditating on future plans, Vida proposes that on their return the librarian-narrator should leave his job: 'We're going to fix you up with a new life' (*A*, p. 129). The suggestion is that the 'hero's' departure from the library is, in fact, a birth into real life, and that his past existence among and in books has been a kind of (very unpainterly) 'still life'. This becomes more than merely an implication when the narrator ends up in Tijuana, describing (in a style close to that of the most elusive passages of *In Watermelon Sugar*) not one abortion but *three*, which he successively labels not 'her . . .' but 'my first', 'my second', 'my third'. If this conceit is not an arbitrary one, its obvious association is with the three preceding books that 'Richard Brautigan' has written. After all, the librarian who lives among 'the beautiful darkness of lives' has talked about 'his' book; and that book, called 'Moose' or 'Buffalo', will remain behind him when he leaves to re-enter life – in the company of a woman who herself has abandoned her unreal beauty (her 'wrong body') to a book that is also to be consigned, stillborn, to the shelves. Of course, to go out into the world might mean becoming a 'cult hero'; and that preoccupation emerges, formally and thematically, to dominate the novel's end, in the section called 'The Hero'. It is underlined in the final sentence: 'Vida was right when she said that I would be a hero in Berkeley' (*A*, p. 226).

It is, indeed, difficult not to read a novel that opens with the mention of previous dead books by a man who is half librarian and half author, and which ends on a similar note, as a form of self-reflexive writing. One might also wonder whether the inferior quality of the scenes that follow the brilliant beginning of a novel that could well have been called 'The Librarian' or 'The Library' is due to the failure to persist with, or to the abortion of, the original idea, and the decision to turn instead to 'romantic possibilities', a generic redirection perhaps exposed in the actual title. If we are to believe what is stated in a poem in *The Pill Versus the Springhill Mine Disaster*, the historical (even dated) part of the text goes against the grain of the plot development chosen for *The Abortion*. What links poem and novel is the shared theme of 'the wrong body' ('"This book is about my body," she said. "I hate it. It's too big for me. It's someone else's body. It's not mine"' (*A*, p. 43); 'Oh, pretty girl, you have trapped / yourself in the wrong body' (*Pill*, p. 16)). To a far greater extent than is at first apparent, the novel begins to deconstruct fixed technical and genre criteria (I shall return to this in Chapter 5). In *The Abortion*, Brautigan initiates the challenge to the credibility of familiar literary genres that will dominate his subsequent books. The contrast between the book's title and subtitle is a 'border scene', like Tijuana itself, a place of kitsch and ambiguity that requires a special taste; 'Border towns are not very pleasant places. They bring out the worst in both countries,' notes the narrator (*A*, p. 155). But it is precisely on such difficult borders that the books that follow will work.

*

The Hawkline Monster (1974) is subtitled 'A Gothic Western', a duplicitous phrase that both debunks and recuperates literary genre. Brautigan's novels, to this point, had been works that demonstrated the confinements of the narrative cage, walks in the prison-house of language where unplanned detours and futile escapes functioned both as attempts at breakout and as tentative affirmations of the possibility of living behind bars. *The Abortion* had suggested a way of escape towards a new subject-matter, together with a new scepticism towards it; *The Hawkline Monster* seems to draw both on the subject and on the scepticism, so that suspicion is well in order as we approach this new 'novel'.

This 'gothic western' begins in Hawaii at the beginning of the twentieth century ('Go further to the west, young man!') but centres around the adventures of two killers, Greer and Cameron, which take place in an isolated house somewhere in mid-Oregon. The book concludes with an abrupt summary of the rest of their lives. One passes from the first, 'western' part, made up of twenty-seven fragments, into the third, 'gothic' part, made up of fifty-six, through the narrow passage of the pompously titled second 'part', composed of a scanty five sections. In that second part, Brautigan merely establishes the bare essentials of the plot, presents the book's 'gothic' premises, and offers us a quick glimpse of the 'monster'. To either side of this section lie two distinct worlds. The first is naturally and objectively attached to the background of the western characters (an Indian girl and two killers) who inhabit it; the second, which Cameron and Greer also seem naturally to inhabit, is the characteristic world of the heroes and heroines of Horace Walpole, Ann Radcliffe and Mary Shelley, the world of gothic. No element of the traditional décor seems missing from either department; two generic worlds are thus populated.

Thus, from the literary props and sets department, Brautigan provides, for his first part, a stagecoach, cowboys, rented horses and a feud between farmers; for the second part, stylish furniture, tawdry trinkets, high-collared dresses, 'scientific' garbs, high-ceilinged rooms and an impeccable butler. The western saloon belongs to the sheriff, and Mark Twain; the Fall of the House of Hawkline would bring a satisfied smile to Edgar Allan Poe. Everything is in place, from spurs to cut mirrors. Admittedly the Hawkline sisters are not particularly shy or maidenly, and Widow Jane, at the stagecoach stop, pushes western hospitality to unaccustomed extremes; but, beyond such minor, parodic variations, the discourse is homogeneous and the components familiarly positioned. Finally, so that all may be clear, characters who complement each other in the text will tend to look alike. Thus, in passing from western to gothic, the Indian girl Magic Child will merely change clothes in order to start becoming Miss Hawkline – one of the two Miss Hawklines, that is; but in the gothic world of doubles the two are indistinguishable. By the same token, save for a few distinct linguistic traits, the two killers could well be brothers. Indeed, the more characters change in situation, the more they look alike. The image of the mirror, under which the monster makes its first appearance, reinforces this pattern of similitude and opposition.

Nothing, we are thus told, really differs between the western and the gothic; characters from one category belong equally well under the laws of the other. Their artificial, coded lives are invariable, their discourse identical. Greer has trouble in expressing himself but has no need to worry, since 'The right words found him'; he thus joins a series of characters who are acted out by being acted on, performing the parts they have been dealt. Each knows what he or she is able to say, or has to say; the laws of the genre function in a closed circuit, generating their own apt images: 'Cora, the barbed-wire drummer, had dozed off. He looked like a sleeping fence' (*HM*, p. 35). Violence and death being the accepted climate here, the appropriate similes are inevitable: the Dead Hills 'looked as if an undertaker had designed them from leftover funeral scraps' (*HM*, p. 57); and Brautigan also links the end of writing to death – 'The road was very bleak, wandering like the handwriting of a dying person over the hills. . . . the road . . . was barely legible' (*HW*, p. 57). Everything is fixed in advance, and therefore one can define landscape and décor negatively, by inverting the references to a well-known norm: the town of Billy *doesn't* have a hotel or a bank; this bridge does *not* have a hanged man suspended from it; Hawaii is *not* in its usual place. The landscape owes so much to Stephen Crane's 'Blue Hotel' or 'The Bride Comes to Yellow Sky' that the name Cora (that of Crane's common-law wife) has total fictional appropriateness.

On the other side of the mirror, in the land of the gothic, the same rules appear to apply. The vast fireplaces and the damasked sofas ought to ensure the stability of the décor, though the daring language of the Hawkline sisters does seem to question it. But this is the darker side of the novel, where things do not have the schematic simplicity of the western. There is something rotten in the kingdom of the gothic, as there always is; therefore, in all logic, a monster dwells in the house.

By comparison, the western of the first part is pure, for all the parodic notes. Brautigan tells us that the two killers 'didn't put any lace on their killing', as they should not, since lace and all such decorations belong in the other, gothic world. In the world of Greer and Cameron, simplicity and rusticity reign; one simply kills whomever 'needs killing', and death does not provoke any special emotion ('Finally they came across something human. It was a grave'; *HM*, p. 59). *The Hawkline Monster* could, to start with, be a regular western, untroubled by any extraneous elements or heretical events:

> At one time Greer thought he saw something different but he was mistaken. What he saw was exactly the same as what he had been seeing. He thought it was smaller but then he realized it was exactly the same size as everything else. (*HM*, p. 61)

Anything left indefinite simply accrues to the genre at work; so Brautigan need not describe to us the exact nature or physiognomy of the two killers, since they are 'the same as in western books or films'. The fact that they can communicate with minimal expression simply means that their messages are ineluctable; Cameron merely counts what words are too complex to express, for a simple reality can easily be recorded and listed in neat columns. So the flat world of the western is reproduced seamlessly, in its utter platitude, concentrated and freeze-dried. It stays flat and horizontal, as compared to the gothic verticality of Book 3, where strangeness and distortion are appropriate. Greer and Cameron do not immediately understand the word 'supernatural', but it demands admission. From cellar to attic, the house displays its Piranesian labyrinths and lines. There is a strict respect for all the expected décor and atmosphere, but one soon notices that an unusual presence haunts and troubles the world of gothic discourse itself. Somewhere in the borderland between Twain, Poe and Crane, something has been born which progressively warps the normal progression of American fiction, a strange force that shakes the perpendicular bars of the two dominant genres and modes of discourse in search of its freedom.

Indeed, the gothic universe of the Hawklines has scarcely been entered when strange phenomena occur. One of the killers, we are told, 'didn't like his mind fucked around with', but Miss Hawkline, more soberly, has to admit: 'Something happened to our minds in the kitchen' (*HM*, p. 95). The four characters have hardly got acquainted round an improvised meal of welcome than conversation becomes mysteriously difficult; mental confusion reigns, and it is suddenly impossible to shake loose words that are alien to the conversation at hand. The characters are stricken with closure through repetition, and they cannot avoid progressing in circles, misunderstanding everything or taking one word for another, repeating sentences already uttered, introducing totally superfluous or inadequate phrases into the discussion. The circularity is contagious, and it prolongs a latent tendency of Greer's ('Greer thought about having another piece of pie but he didn't. It was a nice thought. He really liked the pie and the thought was as good as having another piece of pie. The pie was that tasty'; *HM*, p. 48). Even the narrative voice succumbs, repeating things from Book 1, and there is no diegetic advance at all for several 'chapters'. All kinds of exhortation and self-encouragement are required to pull the narrative out of the rut ('Anyway: on with the story') until the machinery of story begins to grip again. But now the bizarre has its hold; strange events have begun to happen, ever since, as the Hawkline sisters explain, the monster appeared. Characters and things have proved unstable, out of character, out of function. Strange and fanciful manifestations abound: green feathers have found their way into shoes, objects move about, both sisters have ended up naked for no reason at all, and, worse, in a world in which duplication, reflection, reproduction and resemblance are the generic norm, the 'strange occurrences' 'seldom duplicate themselves'. Surprises abound to the point where the narrative voice – which has from the beginning of the book steadily and proleptically announced the major events in expected sequence – has to admit its own astonishment. As Cameron puts it: 'What the fuck next?' (*HM*, p. 142).

An explanation is afforded: it is Professor Hawkline's experiments on mysterious 'chemicals' in his basement laboratory which have triggered off this disastrous situation. Now he has disappeared, and nothing is as it should be. From this point on, one begins reading *The Hawkline Monster* as an allegory, and indeed most of the events of the book go on to confirm this emphasis. A craftsman who works on traditional discourses elaborated in experiments on language, Professor Hawkline (who hawks lines about?) suddenly discovers that his activity is threatened by an infinitely more powerful creative force, uncontrollable, wild, protesting against and denouncing every norm, even those of the gothic to which it rightfully belongs – a monster. The organization and distribution of space in the book's physical environment gives a psychological basis to such a reading: the superstructures of the house neatly correspond to the finished product, which is discursive narration, and the basement to the place where language is seen as tool and vehicle, where words as ingredients are worked on, while, yet deeper still, surging up from below, comes language as matter, as active force, as desire, as the movement and substance of the poetic urge. As Greer clearly puts it, in the empire of this monster 'The Chemicals can change your thoughts around in your head and also steal the clothes right off your body' (*HM*, p. 105). So the word 'naked', when substituted for the word 'clothed', is sufficient to strip the clothes from Miss Hawkline – a very literal proof of what we commonly call 'the power of words', which is what Brautigan's elaborate argument is concerned with.

The house becomes the House not of the Seven Gables but of the Four Languages, and again text opposes discourse. The two ruling genres – one western and one gothic, one too hot, the other too cold – prove equally arid and unproductive, and contrast with the jovial creativity of a free Eugenspiegel-like language. In the world reduced to dysfunction by words that refuse to follow the rules of the game, the characters become lost. They are unable to recognize things seen only shortly before, and the story cannot make any progress, as the text constantly invites it to pause, digress, return, loop back and frolic ('This conversation about the elephant foot umbrella stand had all the markings of the kind of stuff the monster would pull off'; *HM*, p. 187). The monster, that small light which its shadow (reason? narrative logic?) has trouble in following, thus wields the only power that matters: 'did it not have the power to change objects and thoughts into whatever form amused it?' (*HM*, p. 189). Readers and characters alike become victims of imagination and fantasy, who can themselves only follow and 'perform the perfunctory tasks of a shadow'. Meanwhile, upstairs in the house, the language of dialogue has been damagingly hit, and grows poorer every minute:

> Just then there was a knock at the front door. . . .
> 'What's that?' Greer said.
> 'It's somebody knocking at the door,' Cameron said. . . .
> 'It's the butler,' the other Miss Hawkline said. . . .
> 'The butler?' Greer said.
> 'Yes, the butler,' the other Miss Hawkline said. (*HM*, p. 107)

The gothic discourse which is supposed to govern here can no longer rule. Cameron cannot recognize the romantic prints *à la* Udolpho that hang on the walls, and the twin sisters cannot integrate the language into their system of references, causing the two killers to object to the sisters' disregard for their present plight. Thus the 'chemicals' have made their effect felt upstairs, contaminating the quality of life in the house: 'the monster was an illusion created by a mutated light in The Chemicals, a light that had the power to work its will upon mind and matter and change the very nature of reality to fit its mischievous mind' (*HM*, p. 129).

So the verbal utilitarianism of discourse is radically questioned and disrupted by the subversive power of the poetic imagination.

> It started off with the professor finding black umbrellas in unlikely places in the laboratory and green feathers scattered

about and once there was a piece of pie suspended in the air and the professor took to thinking too long about things that were not important. (*HM*, pp. 127–8)

By the same token, the exotic fantasy of Brautigan's pseudo-thriller, *Dreaming of Babylon*, acts as a creative sequel suspended from an impoverished genre that has delivered all it could and just 'lies there', exhausted and bloodless. The past harmony of the generic literary codes, where functions were clearly established, roles neatly distributed, is over. Characters no longer pretend they control the text; words act them out and establish the real links and structures of the book. Novelistic 'action' and 'plot' must temporarily let in textual deep springs, for the monster's 'powers of dark invention had just barely been tapped'. This is why, with the tacit complicity of a shadow, which must follow the light, discursive artefacts will collude but also react, destroying what has brought about an unacceptable situation. Thus the monster makes the Hawkline sisters 'do things that were completely out of character. The transformation of one Hawkline sister into an Indian, the shadow thought, was a very gross deed' (*HM*, p. 173). Aware of the damage a free-roving text is capable of, this persistent shadow – the narrator shadow, the reason shadow, the shadow that is accomplice to the traditional laws of genre – prefers to work towards that text's disappearance, even if this means that the shadow dies too: 'The shadow wished that the Hawkline Monster were dead, even though it would probably have to follow the monster into oblivion' (*HM*, p. 174). When language threatens to escape all control, the killers must move in, to perform an act of public safety, restoring everything to 'normal'. After the spell is broken, Professor Hawkline reappears to draw the inescapable lesson, 'Never again'; the chemicals and the monster are too dangerous.

The Lazarus-like resurrection of the Professor is, however, paid for, by the classic gothic destruction of his work. The Fall of the House of Hawkline results, in classic fashion, from the melting of its ice foundations as a consequence of the fire caused by the monster's death. Only the characters survive, and their destiny undergoes a prodigious acceleration, as a result of a rhetorically stale and traditionally melodramatic epilogue that is now free from the poetic monster which had been preventing it from functioning. But essential questions have been raised and, as Brautigan discloses, before he allows the novelistic discourse to complete its final act of mummification, and as he sits his characters down on the lawn by the newly created lake:

> The way everybody was sitting it looked as if they were at a picnic but the picnic was of course the burning of a house, the death of the Hawkline Monster and the end of a scientific dream. It was barely the Twentieth Century. (*HM*, p. 210)

The text might have lost its battle, but not the war itself. There is still the century to come, and, even though the monster is dead, the text may well be organizing its defences, along the lines the monster unsuccessfully attempted:

> The Hawkline Monster . . . waited, contemplating what form of action to follow next. It tried to realize a container, a shape to put its magic and its spells in and then to evoke that container upon these people who threatened its existence. (*HM*, p. 183)

This particular attempt may have ended, once more, in fixity and impotence, but the problem of evolving new genres and new shapes remains, and the search for forms of poetic and literary subversion continues.

5

STRIP(UNDER)MINING

'By the way,' Doc Edwards said. 'How's that book coming along?'
'Oh, it comes along.'
'Fine. What's it about?'
'Just what I'm writing down: one word after another.'
'Good.' (*In Watermelon Sugar*)

The collapse of the traditional genre distinctions is one of the most dominant features of Brautigan's work. In *Trout Fishing in America* the narrative evolution of myth is blocked by the introduction of a new discourse, and in *In Watermelon Sugar* two rival discourses struggle throughout for domination. The convergence and collision of different genres provides the dynamics of *The Hawkline Monster* and, later, of *Willard and his Bowling Trophies: A Perverse Mystery* (1974) and *Dreaming of Babylon: A Private Eye Novel 1942* (1977). Just as Donald Barthelme persistently suggests that public languages invade private beings ('Our rhetoric is preserved by our elected representatives. In the fat of their heads'; 'The Explanation', in *City Life* (1970)), so Brautigan sees characters sucked dry of inner life by outward linguistic systems, and pits adversary systems against these. The result is sometimes a method of strategic parody, a mocking and subversion of genres. But this is part of a larger and more precise struggle, which seeks the partial deconstruction of the narrative fundamentals – plot, character, structure – through ellipse, discontinuity, redundancy, *trompe-l'œil*, syntactic disruption. The result is perhaps best distilled in an excellent definition of 'poetic language': 'A practice of contradiction; tension between the rhetoric of a given time, a culturally dated language and a discursive instance whose referentials are I-here-now. The exercise of liberty in the individual-collective relationship.'[9]

Genre in Brautigan hence collapses in many ways. It is hard to make any effective distinctions among his poems, his short stories and his book chapters, for neither the size nor the context of his writing clearly expresses its generic nature. In *Rommel Drives on Deep into Egypt*, '1891–1914' is an entire poem; so is 'Oh, well, call it a / life' (*Rommel*, pp. 27 and 76). The following is not an excerpt from, but the entirety of, a short story: ' "It's very hard to live in a studio apartment in San Jose with a man who's learning to play the violin." That's what she told the police when she handed them the empty revolver' (*RL*, p. 53). Similarly, this is a chapter from a novel: 'Q: What about the Logan sisters? A: Forget them' (*WBT*, p. 167). It is easy to extend this list. Brautigan has always encouraged us to question and doubt the genres; indeed, each of his first publications was described as a 'writing', followed by a number. Likewise, Brautigan insists on the concentric and equal value of those circles he calls chapters, vignettes, poems, lines, verses, sentences, words; he takes them as free units to be used in plural patterns of succession and combination.

Willard and his Bowling Trophies (1974) is a curious mixture of erotic narrative and detective novel, in which the disappearance of the Logan brothers' bowling trophies – together with their apparently accidental presence in a couple's apartment (where the trophies share a room with Willard, a papier-mâché bird) – connects the spasmodic actions of a number of sketchy characters. The book emphasizes the autonomy of fragments. Bob is reading the *Greek Anthology*, a herbarium of quotes, much as Brautigan's 'novels' are herbaria of images:

'These are just fragments. Lines,' he said. 'Parts of lines and sometimes only single words that remain from the original poems written by the Greeks thousands of years ago.'
  ' "More beautiful," ' Bob said. 'That's all that's left of a poem.'

'"Having fled,"' Bob said. 'That's all that's left of another one.'

'"He cheats you,"' Bob said. '"Breaking." "You have made me forget all my sorrows." There are three more.'

'Here are two really beautiful ones,' Bob said. '"Deeply do I mourn, for my friends are nothing worth." "Take bites of the cucumbers."' (*WBT*, pp. 24–5)

Bob constantly reads fragments, while Brautigan uses his action to generate them. The title of the chapter is one of the fragments quoted, and the last one Bob quotes here has a programmatic implication: 'And nothing will come of anything' (*WBT*, p. 25). When this is repeated three pages and two chapters later as a title, what seems to be demonstrated is that something can indeed come out of nothing.

Thus Brautigan's style persistently works towards fragmentation – a feature equally evident in his use of the larger markers of a book, its 'parts' or 'chapters'. Brautigan uses such segmentations and separations, dividing his books into 'books' or 'parts', but these do not function to produce generic regularity either; apart from *The Hawkline Monster*, where the organization does support a strongly directional plot, the divisions are not primary parts of the narrative sequence. Essential themes are constantly announced in what seems a totally incoherent order, so that the reader feels that the chapter order is not of paramount importance, and may well come to doubt the value of all such logical and chronological sequences. Section titles become part of the fragmentation. So in *Willard and his Bowling Trophies* there are two chapters entitled 'Events Leading Up to the' and 'Theft of the Bowling Trophies'; they seem to be logically connected, but they are not. For such titles mirror, refract or reverse: 'Willard, the Bowling Trophies and Greta Garbo' (*WBT*, p. 43) leads to the later 'Greta Garbo and Willard' (*WBT*, p. 84). As Brautigan puts it, they 'echo' (so the title 'Matthew Brady' on p. 109, 'The Matthew Brady Echo' on p. 119). Titles produce their own circular structure, like the 'Margaret' titles in *In Watermelon*

Sugar ('Margaret Again', 'Margaret Again, Again', etc.); they become systems of stylistic slippage. There is one title-sequence that seems to function strongly – namely, that to do with the theft of the bowling trophies. But even this is subject to permutation. When the Logan brothers realize the trophies are gone, Brautigan builds a group of images round the instant:

> The Logan family stood in a half-circle around the cabinet not believing their eyes. They were silent miniature Mount Rushmores.
>
> 'SOMEBODY STOLE OUR BOWLING TROPHIES!!!' finally broke the silence like a locomotive leaping its tracks and crashing into an ice-covered lake to sink instantly out of sight, leaving a giant steaming hole in its wake. (*WBT*, pp. 59–60)

But when, a few pages later, we reach the shortest chapter in the book, which reads 'OH, GOD! THE BOWLING TROPHIES ARE GONE!', it is a fragment from the larger image that ascends to title status: the chapter is called 'Locomotive Bubble' (*WBT*, p. 65). The divisions and segments of conventional writing are thus endowed with superficial functions, challenging their representational purpose.

From this process, the entire logic of a book can proceed. So the novel *Willard and his Bowling Trophies* starts with two epigraphs, referring to its structural confrontation between the erotic and the violent. By the end the two fragments interact: Anacreon's 'The dice of Love are madnesses and melees', referring to the opening scenes of eroticism and perversity, collapses into Senator Frank Church's 'This land is cursed with violence', which corresponds with the later action:

> ' "The dice of Love are madnesses and melees," ' Bob quoted from the *Greek Anthology* as the Logan brothers kicked in the front door and ran into the apartment looking for the bowling trophies and the first one in ran down the hall into the bedroom shouting, 'BOWLING TROPHY THIEVES DIE!' and shot the two people, one of whom was sitting on the bed

reading from a book while the other one was lying in bed, listening to him as he read with her eyes closed. (*WBT*, p. 166)

In reading Brautigan one steps out of a classical or Cartesian universe; logic exists, but it is applied only to the imaginative, not to the intellectual process. Traces of classical rhetoric go (it is hard to find a 'since', a 'though' or a 'therefore' in his texts, let alone a 'not only . . . but also'). Orderly grammatical logics give way to parataxis – that is to say, the presentation of clauses without intervening causal connectives – a grammatical trope that is in fact a recurrent feature of much de-causalized contemporary writing. Brautigan's sentences aspire to autonomy – as if they wanted to ensure their own survival when their surrounding context has collapsed. In this, Brautigan is the most consistent practitioner of fragmentary prose there is, since he constantly reduces prose to its most fundamental constitutive unit. Few of his sentences have more than one or two clauses, and these are usually simply hinged on an 'and' or a 'but'. Indeed, Brautigan would clearly rather dispense with co-ordinating words altogether, and let punctuation do the work; one thinks of the fascination exerted by Ecclesiastes on Jesse in *A Confederate General* –

At first I read it over and over again every night, and then I read it once every night, and then I began reading just a few verses every night, and now I was just looking at the punctuation marks. Actually I was counting them, a chapter every night. . . . I was doing it as a kind of study in engineering.

Certainly before they build a ship they know how many rivets it takes to hold the ship together and the various sizes of the rivets. I was curious about the number of rivets and the size of those rivets in Ecclesiastes, a dark and beautiful ship sailing on our waters. (*CG*, p. 75)

Brautigan's sentences, while they move towards fragmentary effect, display the utmost simplicity. Brautigan never ceases to practise the elementary clarity he had recommended in *Please Plant This Book*, where he seeks to master the unit of the sentence for use in the dross-laden world of fiction: 'The time is right to mix sentences with / dirt and the sun with punctuation and rain with verbs' ('Squash', *PPTB*). Instead of conventional subordinates, he places great dependence on the link 'like'. Object pronouns are seldom used to replace substantives, which retain their own valence and promote parataxis, as here:

> Moths fluttered above the light that came out of the river from the tombs below. There were five or six moths fluttering over each tomb.
>
> Suddenly a big trout jumped out of the water above a tomb and got one of the moths. The other moths scattered and came back again, and the same trout jumped again and got another moth. He was a smart old trout.
>
> The trout did not jump any more and the moths fluttered peacefully above the light coming from the tombs. (*IWS*, p. 26)

Thus embossed on trivial structures, vocabulary and imagery multiply their power of suggestion.

*

It is in these methods of selection rather than combination that we find some of the essential roots of Brautigan's poeticity. His unending struggle with the conventional discourse of the novel is enhanced by the sophisticated simplicity of his linguistic structures: such a minimal use of systematic combination places us on the borders of collage, closer to the plastic arts than to a conventional novel. Informed by an acute sense of the moment, the power of the instant (as we shall see later), Brautigan's syntax represents a fundamental choice, in favour of a *being-here* of speech – as opposed to the novel's habitual *having-been*. Brautigan does not tell, or retell, stories; we are emphatically in the presence of a narrative that is always being made. His fiction always pushes forward, feels into the coming moment – unlike realistic fiction, which is regularly slowed down and held back by the weight of an implied past, a previous world of events that must be retold. In his work, writing is always being *done something to*; it eludes the constraint of an *a priori* set of references that determine the nature of the narrative progression. We learn to follow not the 'story-line' but the motif, to take tangents, to play truant: 'Connections proliferate, meanings drop away.'[10] Modulations of similes and lexical devices form the dominant set of harmonics, in which the meaning inheres. And, as time has gone on, Brautigan seems to have increased the frequency and length of his escapes from predetermined narrative, moving further away from the past tense and stripping his fiction of all but a minimum of 'tellable' events. The early books (*A Confederate General, Trout Fishing, The Abortion* and much of *The Revenge of the Lawn*) are filled with reminiscences and with scenic wealth; the more recent books (*In Watermelon Sugar, The Hawkline Monster, Willard and his Bowling Trophies, Dreaming of Babylon, Sombrero Fallout*) are virtually devoid of dramatic action. If we try to find the break, it seems to lie between 1966 and 1970. The poetry of *Rommel*, published in 1970 in the year of *The Abortion*, affords a clue as he ponders on the next choice: 'All secrets of past tense have just come my way, / but I still don't know what I'm going to do / next' (*Rommel*, p. 25).

Curiously, it may well be that it is just these features which account for Brautigan's great popularity, for his techniques of luminous simplicity bring him close to what still remains the most popular form of expression: the visual image. Indeed, his stylizations relate his writings very closely to the methods of that key form of narrative, the strip cartoon. During the 1930s Nathanael West sought to write novels resembling comic strips, and in 1969 Ronald Sukenick observed: 'Once comic books imitated fiction. Soon we're going to have fiction like comic strips',[11] while Kurt Vonnegut and others have incorporated comic-strip-like cartoonings into some of their more recent work. The resemblance in Brautigan's work does not

simply lie in his integration of familiar comic-strip devices —
like the cry of the alligator in *A Confederate General*, the ironic
'Arfwowfuck! Noisepoundpoundpoundpoundpoundpound!
POUND! POUND!' of the deer running round the vortex of an
outhouse in *Trout Fishing in America*, or the two-page
'RRRRRRRRIIIIIIIIINNNNNNNNGGGGGGGG!' of *Willard and his
Bowling Trophies*. The more important connection is his liking
for, and use of, comic-strip methods of figurative narration: a
sense of scenic distribution, certain methods of diegetic
arrangement and a use of redundant forms (which will be
analysed below).

Indeed, his works abound in references to pictorial processes
— not only to actual comic strips, but to photography, films and
television (the 'video pacifier' of *Revenge of the Lawn*). Pictur-
ing things is thus crucial, and analogies with painting are
frequently made; many of the titles of his chapters are like the
titles of paintings. Even his constant references to statues,
mirrors and ice link him with the supercool methods of the strip
cartoon: these moments solidified in frozen frames reveal two
essential elements of Brautigan's art — distance and instant-
aneousness. As will be pointed out in Chapter 6, much of
Brautigan's work is concerned with fixing the instant and
contemplating it; in order to avoid mourning its death, it is held
at arm's length. What seems to be in apparent contradiction
with his fear of narrative fixity is, indeed, when it comes to
dealing with time and figuration, the positive facet of an
ambiguous fascination: where merely spatial fixity is reminiscent of death, an urge to arrest the instant reveals a desire to
stop time's irresistible movement towards death. Ironically, the
cult of the instant generates conventional presentations of the
fixed and controlled as indestructible fragments of life. At the
same time, immobilization is a sound satirical method of
debunking plots, characters and even literary genres.

The slowness of Brautigan's plots tends towards stasis; one
passes from slow motion, via fixed shots, to the static unit of
the photograph, the still:

I left the lantern on and stared at the shadows in the room.

They were rather nice shadows for a time that was so ominous, that drew so near and all enclosing. I was so sleepy now that my eyes refused to close. The lids would not budge down. They were statues of eyes. (*IWS*, p. 83)

Into such 'statues' are changed, from time to time, most of the characters of *Willard and his Bowling Trophies*. Willard himself is one, an intermediary between people and trophies, things congealed into a shape or role. A couple makes '*immortal* love in the bedroom' (*WBT*, p. 109; my italics); the photographer Matthew Brady haunts the novel, just as he did the battlefields of the Civil War, immobilizing instants that would otherwise go unrecorded. As the soldiers in war, so the characters in books: 'They all played out their parts perfectly' (*WBT*, p. 110). Actors are petrified, and then start to move again when the 'camera' shifts from the end of one chapter to the beginning of the next, moving from image to image. 'Statues of Logan brothers' listen to the telephone's two-page ring (*WBT*, pp. 105–6) and then, in 'Marble to Flesh', 'The marble hand of the Logan brother beside the telephone suddenly became living flesh and he picked up the telephone' (*WBT*, p. 111). Nearly all his characters suffer these moments of iconic arrest to their existence, or are fixed in permanent functions. The narrator of *Revenge of the Lawn*, in a bank, has 'to stand there and endure the financial crucifixions of America'; living and dead forms coexist in the cinema in the same book:

Just then the dog in the cartoon let go with a huge yawn because the chicken was still keeping him awake and before the dog had finished yawning, the man next to me started yawning, so that the dog in the cartoon and the man, this living human being, were yawning together, partners in America. (*RL*, p. 100)

Thus, like many contemporary novels, Brautigan's fictions contain very few 'characters' in the conventional sense. His agents are rather what Greimas calls 'actants', what we might term 'expressers of discourse'. Characters are complete prisoners of their role. Working against the tradition of realism, his

73

novels make the characters act and then replace them with a mere sign of their activity:

> The comic-book-reading Logan brother put the comic book down on the bed beside him.
> The beer-drinking Logan brother finished one beer and started on another one. . . .
> The pacing Logan brother was walking up and down the tiny room. (*WBT*, p. 39)

In *A Confederate General*, the 'rich queer' never departs from this nominative definition, remaining a 'rich queer' from the beginning to the end of the chapter ('The first time I met Lee Mellon') in a manner reminiscent of Cami's popular novels, with their apparatus of 'obsequious servants' and 'courageous squires', or of Calvino's 'cloven viscount' and 'inexistent knight'. The style itself activates incompetent characters and gives them dubious existence. When we read 'Their future was America and three long years of searching and a process of gradual character disintegration' (*WBT*, p. 82), two versions of the word 'character' may be heard. Their inexistence, or, at least, their appalling mental and spiritual poverty, is translated into a text that jerks them about like puppets ('So they could go on with the rest of their lives together'). The Logan father 'specializes in transmissions' to such an extent that his only task is to serve as a relay between irreconcilable parts of the text. Rather than displaying his characters to us, Brautigan leaves them in the text to vegetate, so that we inspect them as at the zoo or at Madame Tussaud's – while the author as guide reminds us of preceding scenes in which they had acted, or announces a coming role in future scenarios. They grow interchangeable; in *Willard and his Bowling Trophies* the two couples, housed one above the other in the same building, become counterparts, and they have even exchanged their door numbers to emphasize this equivalence. Brautigan takes this even further by introducing into the same book a set of characters, the Logan sisters, whom he never 'uses', repeatedly telling us of their remarkable gifts, yet reaching the last page without really having brought them in. Then a coda invites the reader to 'Forget them'; unused cogs in the narrative machine, they are given back to another sort of 'wrecking yard' after the novelist has explored their fictional possibilities and then let them go – like a clockmaker returning your watch along with a bag containing the 'superfluous' springs and screws.

The comic strip is static; it moves from frame to frame. Fiction's technical equivalent for this is, for Brautigan, the passage from one fixed instant to another constituted by the jump from one image, or chapter, to the next. Obsessed by circularity and fixity, conscious that reality solidifies as soon as thought about, written or drawn, Brautigan uses the method for recovery: his motion from comic-strip square to comic-strip square is a means of saving writing from death. Over-coded dialogues extend this resemblance; like the 'balloons' that carry the words in cartoons, 'said' is codified as a sign of expression, used as the sole formula to attach to the words of his speakers. Similarly, his chapters often open with assertive indicators resembling the passages of text intruded into silent films or boxed in above cartoon frames: 'On my way to the shack . . .', 'Three years later', 'the next morning', 'Nothing was said for ten minutes'. Most important of all, Brautigan frequently uses a key technique of comic-strip presentation: redundancy, or narrative excess. On top of the near-total evacuation of object pronouns and the constant repetition of substantives, Brautigan often seems to add to and decorate his text, tacking direct commentary on to objective description:

Lee Mellon didn't have much of a Southern accent.
   'You don't have much of a Southern accent,' I said. (CG, p. 27)

they stopped two people behind us, a young man and woman, and asked them what nationality they were and they said Italian.
   'We're Italians.' (A, pp. 159–60)

I had my arm around Vida. She was all right but she was a little weak.

'How do you feel, honey?' I said.

'I feel all right,' she said. 'But I'm a little weak.' (*A*, p. 199)

It is a method that may well help to account for Brautigan's present reputation: just as comic strips, with their 'rich and facile message',[12] have long been thought minor art because of the association of the genre with its worst products, so Brautigan's fiction suffers from its being outwardly 'easy' and flip.

*

Mirrors in Brautigan's work provide the only official (if somewhat pathetic) 'movement', which the mind seizes upon in a 'reflection', imagining that the body travels towards its image, but forgetting that the image merely confirms immobility and closure. The narrator of *In Watermelon Sugar* lives in a universe so circumscribed that the future can be seen 'in the Statue of Mirrors'. In this way, space confines time; only fleeting instants, in tiny units, can survive. Brautigan takes us through a gallery of figural moments, iconic florilegia of life in America, discourses divided into immovable categories: 'I found three pictures that were the right flavors: a monster picturehelphelp [*The Hawkline Monster?*], a cowboy picturebangbang [*A Confederate General?*] and a dime store romance pictureIloveyou [*The Abortion?*]' (*CG*, p. 45).

Brautigan's novels assemble on the page battered residues of reality, fragments of coloured glass, the dead leaves of defunct discourse. His art, like that of the cinema, is an art of ellipse and breakage; his aesthetic, even more so than comic strips, is an aesthetic of the discontinuous.

The staccato eventfulness of the novels bears witness to their brutal artificiality. Plausible 'happenings' are thrown at the reader, but the narrative voice eludes them, taking refuge in exploring the interstices of the text. The arbitrary nature of the novel's conventions are thus dismantled. If the traditional attraction of narrative lies in a progressive chronological development resolved into an artfully contrived denouement, if the skilful narrator of such novels is an expert in provoking expectation and prolonging suspense, procuring a final pleasure by producing solutions to the problems that have been carefully contrived, then Brautigan frankly exposes all the contents of the novelist's bag of tricks, while consenting to use them, if haphazardly. 'What about Willard and his bowling trophies? How do they figure into this tale of perversion? Easy. They were in an apartment downstairs' (*WBT*, p. 26). So there. Do you want more? 'Where were the police?' (*SF*, p. 89). 'Where were they? That's simple enough. Dead' (*SF*, p. 101). Any more questions? 'Why were the police dead? That's an easy one' (*SF*, p. 105); and so on.

Brautigan's display is amusing, but it is also essentially analytical; it is both an assertion and a frustration of story. Frustration occurs in one of three main ways. One is that Brautigan constantly displays in advance events that are still to come, as he does in *In Watermelon Sugar* (pp. 8–9); another is the promise, often without satisfaction, that unclear problems will be analysed later ('this will be gone into'; *IWS*, p. 2); another is the simple defusing of all suspense (I might as well tell you now). Unresolved matters accumulate, as if the novel were unable to answer the poetic questions it raises:

> She was lost from him, and he thought about the *Greek Anthology* and remembered words from ancient times that said, 'Painting a lion from the claw.'
>
> What did it mean to him thinking about that as he rested upon her, trying to make love? What good would it do him to think of things like that?
>
> He didn't know. (*WBT*, p. 42)

And *why* did the temperature of the sombrero of *Sombrero Fallout* (1976) rise? *Why* did the corpse in *Dreaming of Babylon* (1977) have to be removed? Brautigan performs the role of the novelist, as a kind of act of 'good faith', but he also undermines that role at the deepest level. Held in stasis, arbitrarily raising and denying promises and pleasures, his

77

books end on exits rather than resolutions. One thinks of the sculptor's confession to his friend in *In Watermelon Sugar*:

'How's it coming?' she said.
'It's finished,' I said.
'It doesn't look finished,' she said.
'It's finished,' I said. (*IWS*, p. 67)

Statues and books can be left dead and finished anywhere. The only real thing that could give them life is dynamite.

6

THE REEL WORLD

We live but a little, in each instant, of what the instant proposes. And yet all we live is the instant itself, and the instant itself is but what we live of it. We have to become penetrated with 'the total equality of the present instant and of the real'. (Jean Lescure, Afterword to Gaston Bachelard, *L'Intuition de l'instant* (1965))

Just as the author, since he has no intention of telling about himself, decided to call the character 'I' as if to conceal him, not having to name him or describe him, because any other name or attribute would define him more than this stark pronoun; still, by the very fact of writing 'I' the author feels driven to put into this 'I' a bit of himself, of what he feels or imagines he feels. Nothing could be easier for him than to identify himself with me; for the moment my external behaviour is that of a traveller who has missed a connection, a situation that is part of everyone's experience. (Italo Calvino, *If On a Winter's Night A Traveller* (1981))

In 1980, two years after his ninth collection of poems, *June 30th–June 30th*, Brautigan published his ninth novel, *The Tokyo–Montana Express*, a work that seems to mark a point of pause and meditation in Brautigan's by now extended development as a man and as a writer. The novel is far closer to being a 'state of the soul' book than any of his previous writings, a work that reflects on his own age and on his past reputation. 'In actuality', he reflects, 'what makes you older is when your bones, muscles and blood wear out, when the heart sinks into oblivion and all the houses you ever lived in are gone and people are not really certain that your civilization ever existed' (*TME*, p. 162). But, if this sense of ageing – of the fading of a set of circumstances and a 'civilization' that was for many people the true source and cause of his writings – makes the book a sad one, none the less a kind of buoyancy is displayed here. The author has weathered the less than sympathetic reviews he had received once the peak of his 'hippie' reputation had been passed; there is increased maturity and control here, though also new doubts and longings. At the same time, these two works of prose and poetry, and the two that preceded them, *Sombrero Fallout* (1976) and *Loading Mercury with a Pitchfork* (1976), demonstrate a return to a poetic spirit close to that of his early endeavours, after the genre wars of his middle period. They are works that have not, in fact, received much critical attention, yet they reveal a great deal about the nature of his achievement as a writer. I want here to look at three neglected aspects of his work, elements that were always present but are particularly apparent in these later writings: the ambiguity of Brautigan's 'I', the time-space in which experience occurs in his world, and his minimalist vision.

It has been argued in this book that Brautigan is what might be called a *novelist of the instant* – a writer much concerned with time within structures of discontinuity, and whose struggle with the linearity of text in fact bears a close resemblance to many ideas in contemporary philosophy. Brautigan's attitude towards philosophical and intellectual utterance has always been somewhat wry, and the authorial 'we' that opens *The Tokyo–Montana Express* writes of being 'cloaked like trick or treaters in the casual disguises of philosophical gossip'. Brautigan is not a philosopher, but his work is consistent with the philosophy of the instant that has been so important a part of contemporary thought – a philosophy in which language itself becomes a centre of ambiguity, paradox and fragility, linear utterance is obstructed, and the presence or absence of the knower becomes an element that modifies the observed situation, generating a doubtful subject, a diaphanous self that lurks in the interstices of being, living, like a Brautigan character, in the immediacy of certain realized instants. 'The deeper our meditation on time penetrates,' Gaston Bachelard has written, 'the lesser it grows. . . . Take a tenuous idea, pull it tight over an instant, it illuminates the mind.' Bachelard also quotes Roupnel:

> Whatever permanence there is in being is the expression not of a motionless and constant cause, but of the juxtaposition of fleeting and unceasing results, each of which has its solitary base, and the linkage of which, a mere habit, composes an individual.[13]

Against the perspectival views of time put forward earlier in the century by Bergson and Guyau, these philosophers stress the constitutive power of *instantaneous* experience and perception, displacing older vitalist and teleological ideas by emphasizing the new insights afforded by the naked, lived intimacy of historyless and unintellectualized thought. The pointed selection of perceptual items ensures the construction – as in the Japanese 'I' novel – of that distinctive unity of tone or deceptive monotony in which the individual mind seems to reveal itself. A return to the freedom of possible successions allows resonances distinct from progressive repetitions. The 'stabilized instant' Baudelaire once explored (Brautigan explicitly takes it up as early as the poems of *The Galilee Hitch-Hiker* (1958)) is one that hesitates always on the very edge of becoming. It chooses addition over development, and replenishment over evolution. Its notes sound in the spirit of modern aesthetics, and they are clearly expressed in the existential and aesthetic import of Brautigan's work.

It is notable that clear chronological limits are set for his most recent novels. *Sombrero Fallout* lasts precisely one hour, and the half-hour is struck in the exact middle of the book. *June 30th–June 30th* proclaims its chosen time-span in the title. *The Tokyo–Montana Express* has the more veiled unit of autobiography, but its unit is the structure of a life-span, itself constituted by a collection of moments, of varying length and intensity, a series of stations invoking both duration and flight:

> Though the Tokyo–Montana Express moves at a great speed, there are many stops along the way. This book is

those brief stations: some confident, others still searching for their identities.

The 'I' in this book is the voice of the stations along the tracks of the Tokyo–Montana Express. (*TME*, p. vii)

The familiar cloak of the indeterminate signified, used in *In Watermelon Sugar* for the narrator, here takes over again from the undefined or polysemic signifier of 'Trout Fishing in America' in *Trout Fishing in America*. The preoccupation with identity that it expresses relays the explicit problematic exposed at the end of the first paragraph quoted above. However, the book's quest cannot be equated with a direct search for a personal self. The collapsing of persona into author, of text into voice, can be justified only once one has established the nature of the quest – which is, in fact, a search for the proper expression of an instant, for the essence of 'the little stretches of imagination I call my brain' (*TME*, p. 101). That instant will be represented by the crystallization and dispersion of a chain of signifiers, and on this all Brautigan's stylistic effects depend. Condensation and displacement govern the text, in much the way that they characterize a dream. Hence the exploration of life proceeds not by sweeping statements and generalizations, but by leaps and bounds from one fraction of time – which summons up one detail – to another. All is drift, through the processes of metaphor, simile and recall; the texture of evanescence is a matter of focus and intensities.

Such is the substance of Brautigan's work: instants, selected by will, or forced on the attention; anecdotes and vignettes; things or objects waiting, in the process of becoming; snapshots; epiphanies; concatenations. Duration is out of the question. Horizontality suggests the superficial and artificial, like metonymic echoes over the void. Only a vertical drilling down into the moment offers access, however problematic, to the truth of existence: '[A wind] through my sleep shaking the branches of my dreams all the way down to the roots of that which I call myself' (*TME*, p. 183). Instants, then, side by side; between them and beyond them, nothingness. As Bachelard has it: 'Absolute naught on both edges of the instant.'[14] Or as Brautigan puts it: 'I find the breaks in his diary very beautiful like long poetic pauses where you can hear the innocence of eternity' (*TME*, p. 6). We have seen this before in his 'writings': in *A Confederate General*, where the pseudo-historical thread is defeated by harmonic proliferation and semantic entropy; in *Trout Fishing in America*, in the selection of moments relived on the 'Calle de Eternidad'; in *In Watermelon Sugar*, which explores iDEATH's timeless space gangrened by inBOIL's history. In later books, 'real stories' are undermined by obstinate stops and stases: 'Later on, when nothing else is happening. I mean, absolutely nothing: zero', in *Dreaming of Babylon (DB*, p. 31); 'Both men's feet were now glued to the ground. They weren't going anywhere. They waited for further developments', in *Sombrero Fallout* (*SF*, p. 61). By the time of *Sombrero Fallout* and *The Tokyo–Montana Express*, these arrests, these refusals to move on, have intensified, producing a fragmented assemblage of places and instants which stand for composition, and seek to increase one's power to penetrate the real by sharpening the focus.

So the eye grows unwilling to meander over panorama; it is moments that drill down into the bedrock of eternity:

> The complicated little life ballet movement started my mind ringing like a sunken bell at the bottom of the Pacific Ocean during a great earthquake tearing cracks in the ocean floor, starting a tidal wave headed toward the nearest shore, maybe thousands of miles away: India. (*TME*, p. 35)

One travels on the surface of time and objects or, as in *Trout Fishing*, 'along the good names'; and one stops here and there to drill in what time there is available ('Seconds'; *LMP*, p. 118). One samples, because 'there isn't enough space in your life to keep everything' (*TME*, p. 149), because 'There's just so much room for so much information here in the Twentieth Century and you have to draw the line someplace' (*TME*, p. 236). Once the poet T. S. Eliot offered to 'show you fear in a handful of dust'; the narrator of *Sombrero Fallout* offers to show the instant of peace, in a single hair.

*

Sombrero Fallout (1976) is a novel about internal strife and dissension. A couple breaks up, an artist breaks down, civil war breaks out. 'America' dictates 'sombrero' to the title, and so does an author accustomed to wearing one; but 'Japanese' (the subtitle of the book is 'A Japanese Novel') dictates 'fallout', remembering Hiroshima and Nagasaki. A well-known American humorist has started writing a story about a sombrero that falls out of the sky into the main street of an American town, but he tears it up, while grieving over the fact that his Japanese girlfriend has left him. America provides the stale discourse, Japan the peripheral textual fallout. The dynamics are those of fission, and concentrated mental atoms release narrative energy. A text, hardly begun, dies: 'He reached into the typewriter as if he were an undertaker zipping up the fly of a dead man in his coffin and removed a piece of paper' (*SF*, p. 12). A half-started narrative thus ends up in the wastepaper basket, but begins to generate another text, which is a metaphor of itself:

> The heart-broken American humorist of course had no idea what was going on among the torn pieces of paper in his wastepaper basket. He did not know that they now had a life of their own and had gone on without him. (*SF*, p. 34)

A cold black sombrero falls out of the sky and remains exactly on the spot where it has fallen. The writer divorces his original creation, his girlfriend having left him. In past life, 'Though he walked slightly in front of her, holding her hand, she was really the guide' (*SF*, p. 55); but, in the narrative present, the text that could not be produced – or led forward – now leads the narrative voice along.

Once writer and story have split, in the first section, two uneven 'dramatic' strands now direct the book. One deals with the writer's tenuous activities in a tight space of time, between 10.15 and 11.15 at night; the other is concerned with the havoc caused by the fall of the sombrero. Both strands seem to represent quite different levels of intensity, but the advance of each is blocked by much the same narrative strategy. Merely staring at the still sombrero brings about pandemonium, but extraordinary mental activity results in the contemplation of a single hair. The two alternating 'plots' generate an interlocking investigation of the relation between reality and the imagination, and they turn into opposite demonstrations of the effect of stasis.

While the humorist simply sits there moping, his imagination roams the fields of the possible, and his mind, turning into 'a popcorn popper over the simplest of things', complicates elementary situations. His imagination feeds on nothingness; phantasms, memory, longing and wishful thinking metamorphose the emptiness of 'now'. All possibilities now become puzzles: his girlfriend is like pieces of a puzzle (*SF*, p. 37), and memories of her seduction are also a puzzle (*SF*, p. 54); his text turns into origami (*SF*, p. 22); his dreams crumble (*SF*, p. 104); his emotions are 'being played through a kaleidoscope of goofiness and insanity' (*SF*, p. 98). Fragments and debris of instants form a textual patchwork quilt which evolves through recurrences, recursions, oppositions and correspondences. As in the dreams of the girlfriend, Yukiko, the real is an absence; but, as the text circles and reels, Yukiko sleeps on, and her dream 'erased itself as it happened' (*SF*, p. 18). So, indeed, does a text that refuses to leave meditative duration for the linear time of diegetic progression – a text that fertilizes itself arbitrarily, turning itself 'into a hundred varieties of his imagination'. After the book's one hour, a hair has been found, lost, and found again – the only thread the humorist hangs on to. Meanwhile the could-bes and might-have-beens excavate and exploit the moment to the point of exhaustion, moving, by a kind of hair-splitting, towards the external minimum. And each new possibility can be reached only after the previous one has been subjected to the treatment of the whisky glass:

'Another one?' the bartender said, looking at the one that was only half-empty in front of him.

'A double,' he said.

The bartender's face remained expressionless because he was a very good bartender. He went and got the whiskey. By the time he was back, the humorist had finished the glass that had been half-full. A minute later the double was half-gone. The humorist with two sips had changed it into a single. (*SF*, p. 39)

In contrast, the 'sombrero' story is ponderously treated. From the appearance of the sombrero onwards, there is no development that merely takes place; each occurrence is announced, taken up, expounded, explained, analysed, denied, transformed, on a never-ending scale that goes from one cold sombrero to a hot national catastrophe. By the application of discursive narrative logic, the sombrero moves from arbitrary object to the source of armed rebellion. While the sad lonely writer seeks to assuage and actually activates the havoc in his mind, the text, from the bottom of its wastepaper basket, operates automatically, moving through clichés to predictable slapstick catastrophes. The humorist may only be able to drill the instant he is living, but 'Meanwhile, in the wastepaper basket', words themselves manage to function as mechanistic story-makers, exposing themselves as pathetic cogs serving discursive narrative machines. Yet all remains still: the lights of San Francisco look to the seated writer 'as if they had been painted on the window', and Yukiko dreams on, 'her long hair reflecting darkness like a mirror'; despite the riot, the sombrero does not move, but simply changes temperature and turns from black to white – the one true 'development' of this 'Japanese', aesthetically exact novel.

*

I was seventeen and then eighteen and began to read Japanese haiku poetry from the seventeenth century. I read Basho and Issa. I liked the way they used language concentrating emotion, detail and image until they arrived at a form of dew-like steel. (*J30*, p. 8)

Thus Brautigan reveals in *June 30th–June 30th* that he has always been attracted to Japanese aesthetics – a mutual attraction, given the success of his books in Japan – and to the linkage through 'perfume, echo and harmony' which Metsuo Basho employed in his 'renga' haiku. This influence is apparent even before we reach Brautigan's more recent work. 'No trespassing / ⁴/17 of a haiku', announces, tongue-in-cheek, the 'Red Lip' chapter of *Trout Fishing in America*. From dew-like steel to steel-like trout and trout-made steel, the same desire to achieve the union of fluidity and formal restriction is apparent. More recent books have displayed the connection less in the form of obvious jokes, more as a calm, crisp meditation. In painting, the technique that would most suit Brautigan is surely that of *la réserve* – that lacuna in the canvas which, unpainted, inscribes absence at the heart of form, while pretending to be ground colour. In the early novels, there were winds, things 'waiting' up the road to eternity, a desire to nullify the landmarks of our knowledge of reality by a quickening of the air between them, intensifying their distance from us ('A trout-colored wind blows / through my eyes, through my fingers'; *Pill*, p. 35). As the novels develop, the colours grow softer, closer to shadows; we discover the perspective of dreams, of insubstantialities; objects, when looked at intently, dissolve and dissipate. Beyond insubstantiality, substance is reached by erecting concrete objects in the mental landscape around which thoughts may play, and by which memories gnaw their way through.

Patient interrogations of the real in its apparently most insignificant manifestations are what enriched haiku when Basho imbued it with the spirit of Zen Buddhism. Likewise in *The Tokyo–Montana Express*: 'I spend a lot of my time interested in little things, tiny portions of reality' (*TME*, p. 188). To consider fleeting feelings before they flee or as they do, the shape of a crow, the blackness of grey, numbers, cans, a blue bucket, being alone, necessitates a slow movement of the mind. Instants become the building blocks of life; lives become units of instantaneous surprises, piled one on top of the other, crisp, contrasted, angular or curvaceous. 'I will turn out to be a phantom memory, and all the lives that she will live', says *Revenge of the Lawn* (p. 110). Microscopic sadnesses and tiny irritations: such simple events in this book become 'the possible telescope for a larger agony' (*RL*, p. 148). Microcosms of pain are as relevant to metaphysical and ontological being as are single objects to the large question of the nature of the real in Wallace Stevens or William Carlos Williams. 'One must keep track of all the small victories,' Brautigan writes in *Revenge of the Lawn* (p. 39), echoing Basho's attachment to finding and unravelling the hidden hopes in small, quotidian things, and so finding 'small specialized forms of happiness' (*RL*, p. 73). 'Dive-bombing the lower emotions', as he puts it in *Loading Mercury with a Pitchfork* (p. 116), opens up the tiny things that matter. In the odd division of labour that exists in human activity, Brautigan recognizes the existence of history and the need for sweeping action (so Kennedy pops into a dream here, Carter and Sadat negotiate there), but he knows where his own responsibilities lie: 'We all have our roles in history. Mine is clouds' (*TME*, p. 150). The shimmer in the grossness of the act, the presence of the volatile in the daily grind, shows what the name of the trade is: it is 'loading mercury with a pitchfork':

> Loading mercury with a pitchfork
> your truck is almost full. The neighbors
> take a certain pride in you. They
> stand around watching. (*LMP*, p. 16)

The reception of his work in Japan undoubtedly encouraged Brautigan to 'continue on in [his] own lonely direction of writing', like, he adds, pointing out the quality of the camouflage, 'a timber wolf slipping quietly through the woods' (*J30*, p. 53). His engagement with Japanese aesthetics is not something simply and fashionably acquired through the Californian popular acceptance of Zen. Brautigan has the decency and humour ('I am that which begins / but has no beginning. / I am also full of shit / right up to my ears'; *J30*, p. 83) not to lean crudely on trendy supports of that sort. The connection is in any case more fundamental. It derives from his desire to rediscover eternal things through the representation of small concrete objects, existing somewhere between gesture and nothingness. In *The Revenge of the Lawn* this had much to do with recovery of the irretrievable past:

> I'm haunted a little this evening by feelings that have no vocabulary and events that should be explained in dimensions of lint rather than words.
>
> I've been examining half-scraps of my childhood. They are pieces of distant life that have no form or meaning. They are things that just happened like lint. (*RL*, p. 121)

More recent writing has been far more conscious of the balance of gains and losses, and knowledge of the spiritual and aesthetic profit within these. So, in *Loading Mercury with a Pitchfork*, 'On pure sudden days like innocence / we behold the saints and their priorities / key-punched in the air' (p. 35), but 'finding is losing something else. / I think about, perhaps even mourn, / what I lost to find this' (*LMP*, p. 32). Or, in *The Tokyo–Montana Express*: 'Everything is here except that which is missing' (*TME*, p. 228). What Brautigan has in mind is the process of selection and inclusion/exclusion in Japanese art, and its pursuit of concentration, the physical and the spiritual grasping of an evanescent reality, that imprint of tail-lights that leaves on film or the retina of the eye the mere trace of a passage:

> Things slowly curve out of sight
> until they are gone. Afterwards
> only the curve
> remains. (*LMP*, p. 107)

And, I might add, the ashes of images that stood for flame and colour. The reel world . . .

One aspect of this process is referred to in *The Tokyo–*

Montana Express, in the passage about Joseph Francl's western diary (to which Brautigan wrote an introduction in 1968): 'His diary is written in a mirror-like prose that is simultaneously innocent and sophisticated and reflects a sense of gentle humor and irony' (*TME*, p. 2). Simplicity is a hard-won thing, and so it is for Brautigan himself – not 'primitivism' but rather a studied minimalism. It is significant that, for a long time, Brautigan felt he could never write the novel he wanted until he knew the secrets of the sentence; the quest for the 'sentence' that he undertook has been apparent throughout this book. In the only (self-) interview with Brautigan we have, he indicated the influential role played by poetry in this: 'I used poetry as a lover but I never made her my old lady.'[15] The superpositioning of his later books, of poetry and fiction, manifests this view of verse as training, a place for the laborious rehearsing of the pleasures of the longer text. At the same time the motionless progression of the prose, and its fundamentally poetic nature, shows the effect. It is a prose of careful reproportioning: 'Too many things were out of proportion in his life in relationship to their real meaning,' he notes in *Sombrero Fallout* (p. 68); and likewise 'his mind translated this into a twelve-ring circus with most of the acts not worth watching a second time. After a while non-stop brilliance has the same effect as non-stop boredom' (*SF*, p. 98). Since there 'is more to life than meets the eye' (*SF*, p. 183), one must examine the hidden side of the very words used in the process of narration itself. We are told in *Sombrero Fallout* that 'this man was so complicated he could make a labyrinth seem like a straight line', for his 'problems were unique and his ability to create new obsessions was awesome' (*SF*, p. 82).

Brautigan's roller-coaster mind takes us on thin threads of narrative drama into strange peaks and dips of language and the imagination; it generates fantastic circuits where the most interesting details are the signs that point out the objects of interest. But beyond the twice-removed reality of the texts, beyond the take-off from the real into the realms of pure feeling which are then transformed into strange lexical equivalents, lies the stubborn demand that, if the real is to be brought to its smallest and stillest components, all faith in discursive meaning must be abandoned, and all obedience to the rules of telling disestablished. In *The Tokyo–Montana Express* we reach the point where the frameless watercolours of pure consciousness depict only still landscapes and dormant waters, the unruffled pregnancies of the painter Hokusai and his so-called 'sabi' equivalents in poetry, with their love of the old, the faded, the unobtrusive.

The Tokyo–Montana Express is a herbarium of interwoven Japanese and American moments, the international and inter-cultural notations of a mind seeking colour and shape as indices of a moment, archives of a season filled with epiphanies and unaccountable disruptions of perception. Brautigan, 47 years old, turns to discover, with astonishment, that such moments – detached, loose in space, unmoving in time – indeed make a life in time. There is a thread linking the various haunting, evanescent and misty spaces he has explored and contemplated, and it is called 'age'. It may be a history of holes vertically drilled in search of meaning and truth, and one will still wonder whether the responses of the moment answer the austere questions of time:

> But I can't change the world.
> It was already changed before I got here.
> Sometimes when I finish writing something, perhaps even this, I feel as if I am handing out useless handbills or I am an old man standing in the rain, wearing shitty clothes and holding a sign for a cabaret that is filled with the beautiful and enticing skeletons of young women that sound like dominoes when they walk toward you coming in the door.
> (*TME*, pp. 206–7)

Yet these salvaged pieces, the instants of a lifetime from boyhood to middle age, proclaim that life so perceived does have a fragmentary unity, and that its bewildering puzzles afford hope and stimulus. And, because he has forsaken the false illusions of transitive existence, and likewise outgrown

91

the literary temptations of parodic indulgence, *The Tokyo–Montana Express* is a work that sounds a clear, loud note of personal recovery – the best work Brautigan has produced since the wonderful original trilogy with which his quest began, that quest from puzzles to epiphanies that this book has explored. It places the random pattern of his stories into a perspective, and it expands the technical potential of previous unautobiographical works. Brautigan's writing has never rendered a prosaic homage to the real; here, however, it proclaims, more clearly and intimately, another potential – the beauty in a 'snowstorm' of two Laurel and Hardy snowflakes (*TME*, p.13), molecular agitations of the still life, Cézanne's *petites sensations*, life arrested by the collapse of duration on to the instant, 'so the wind won't blow it all away', as the title of a Brautigan novel-to-come puts it. Brautigan's works, thin and jumpy, are quiet surfaces of small extent, abruptly breaking into the next frame with enough redundancies and repetitions to validate the plastic equivalent of cartoons and the black paradigmatic strokes lashed on to rice paper. Such work heralds, if Brautigan will allow me, at a time when his critical sun has seemed to set, his 'revenge of the dawn'.[16]

NOTES

1 Harry Levin, *Perspective of Criticism* (Cambridge, Mass.: Harvard University Press, 1963), p. 80.

2 John Barth, 'The Literature of Replenishment', *Atlantic Monthly*, 245, 1 (January 1980), pp. 65–71.

3 Marc Chénetier, 'Harmoniques sur l'irrespect littéraire: Boris Vian et Richard Brautigan', *Stanford French Review*, 1, 2 (Fall 1977), pp. 243–59.

4 *The Overland Journey of Joseph Francl, the First Bohemian to Cross the Plains to the California Gold Fields*, introduction by Richard Brautigan (San Francisco, Calif.: William P. Wreden, 1968). (This is interestingly reviewed by Dale L. Morgan in the *California Historical Society Quarterly*, 49 (1970), p. 72.)

5 This 'message' on the statue in Washington Square has been partly changed, and now reads: 'PO Box with Mementos for the Historical Society, 1979' and 'Time Capsule 1979–2079 AD dedicated to the citizens of San Francisco'! It seems appropriately Brautiganesque that what the statue has to say, from the 1879 dedication to Cogswell onward, changes every hundred years!

6 So in 'Up Against the Ivory Tower', in *Rommel Drives on Deep into Egypt*, the narrator sits in a café, fascinated by a neighbour writing an ordinary address on a mundane envelope, and reflects: 'He's really using the pen.'

7 Jack Hicks, Introduction to *Cutting Edges: Young American Fiction for the Seventies* (New York: Holt, Rinehart & Winston, 1973).

8 See Annie Le Rebeller's interview with John Barth in *Caliban*, 11, 1 (1975), p. 101.

9 Henri Meschonnic and Jean-Claude Coquet, 'Sémiotiques', *Langages*, 31 (September 1973), p. 11.

10 As Ronald Sukenick puts it in his story 'The Birds', in *The Death of the Novel and Other Stories* (New York: Dial, 1969), p. 163.

11 Ibid.

12 Pierre Fresnault-Deruelle, 'Le Verbal dans la bande dessinée', *Communications*, 15 (1970), pp. 145–62.

13 Gaston Bachelard, *L'Intuition de l'instant* (Paris: Gallimard, 1932; repr. 1966).

14 Ibid., p. 154.

15 In *The San Francisco Poets*, ed. David Meltzer (New York: Ballantine Books, 1971), p. 293.

16 Since this essay was written, Brautigan's latest novel has come out in the United States (*So the Wind Won't Blow It All Away*, 1982). Its distinct overtones of reminiscence and meditation amply confirm the orientations delineated in the last chapter of this essay, while bearing out its technical analyses on time and the philosophy of the instant.

BIBLIOGRAPHY
WORKS BY RICHARD BRAUTIGAN

Fiction

A Confederate General from Big Sur. New York: Grove, 1964.
London: Cape, 1971. London: Pan/Picador, 1973.
Trout Fishing in America. San Francisco, Calif.: Four Seasons Foundation, 1967. London: Cape, 1970. London: Pan/Picador, 1972.
In Watermelon Sugar. San Francisco, Calif.: Four Seasons Foundation, 1968. London: Cape, 1970. London: Pan/Picador, 1973.
Revenge of the Lawn: Stories 1962–1970. New York: Simon & Schuster, 1971. London: Cape, 1972. London: Pan/Picador, 1974.
The Abortion: An Historical Romance 1966. New York: Simon & Schuster, 1971. London: Cape, 1973. London: Pan/Picador, 1974.
The Hawkline Monster: A Gothic Western. New York: Simon & Schuster, 1974. London: Cape, 1975. London: Pan/Picador, 1976.
Willard and his Bowling Trophies: A Perverse Mystery. New York: Simon & Schuster, 1974. London: Cape, 1976. London: Pan/Picador, 1980.
Sombrero Fallout: A Japanese Novel. New York: Simon & Schuster, 1976. London: Cape, 1977. London: Pan/Picador, 1978.
Dreaming of Babylon: A Private Eye Novel 1942. New York: Delacorte Press/Seymour Lawrence, 1977. London: Cape, 1978.
The Tokyo–Montana Express. New York: Delacorte Press/Seymour Lawrence, 1980. London: Cape, 1981. London: Pan/Picador, 1982.
So the Wind Won't Blow It All Away. New York: Delacorte Press/Seymour Lawrence, 1982.

Poetry

The Galilee Hitch-Hiker. San Francisco, Calif.: printed by Joe Dunn, White Rabbit Press, 1958.
Lay the Marble Tea. San Francisco, Calif.: Carp Press, 1959.
The Octopus Frontier. San Francisco, Calif.: Carp Press, 1960.
All Watched Over by Machines of Loving Grace. San Francisco, Calif.: Communication Company, 1967.
Please Plant This Book. San Francisco and Santa Barbara, Calif.: Graham Mackintosh, 1968.
The Pill Versus the Springhill Mine Disaster. San Francisco, Calif.: Four Seasons Foundation, 1968. London: Cape, 1970.
Rommel Drives on Deep into Egypt. New York: Delacorte Press/Seymour Lawrence, 1970.

Loading Mercury with a Pitchfork. New York: Simon & Schuster/Touchstone, 1976.
June 30th–June 30th. New York: Dell/Delta, 1978.

Non-fiction

Introduction to *The Overland Journey of Joseph Francl, the First Bohemian to Cross the Plains to the California Gold Fields*. San Francisco, Calif.: William P. Wreden, 1968.
'The Silence of Flooded Houses'. Introduction to *The Beatles' Lyrics*. New York: Dell, 1975.

SELECTED CRITICISM OF RICHARD BRAUTIGAN

Book

Malley, Terence. *Richard Brautigan*. Writers for the Seventies. New York: Warner Paperback Library, 1972.

Articles

Chénetier, Marc. 'Richard Brautigan, écriveur: notes d'un ouvre-boîtes critique'. *Caliban* (Toulouse), 1 (1975), pp. 16–31.
—— 'Harmoniques sur l'irrespect littéraire: Boris Vian et Richard Brautigan'. *Stanford French Review*, 1, 2 (Fall 1977), pp. 243–59.
Clayton, John. 'Richard Brautigan: The Politics of Woodstock'. *New American Review*, 11 (New York: Simon & Schuster, 1971), pp. 56–68.
Critique: Studies in Modern Fiction, 16, 1 (Minneapolis, Minn., 1974). Richard Brautigan special issue.
Loewinsohn, Ron. 'After the (Mimeographed) Revolution'. *Tri-Quarterly* (Spring 1970), pp. 221–36.
Meltzer, David (ed.). In *The San Francisco Poets*, pp. 1–7, 293–7. New York: Ballantine, 1971.
Pétillon, Pierre-Yves. In *La Grand-Route*, pp. 160–8, 236. Paris: Seuil, 1970.
Pütz, Manfred. In *The Story of Identity*, pp. 105–29. Stuttgart: Metzler, 1979.
Schmitz, Neil. 'Richard Brautigan and the Modern Pastoral'. *Modern Fiction Studies* (Spring 1973), pp. 109–25.
Stevick, Philip. 'Scheherazade Runs out of Plots, Goes on Talking, The King, Puzzled, Listens'. *Tri-Quarterly* (Winter 1973), pp. 332–62.
Swigart, Rob. 'Review of *Still Life with Woodpecker* by Tom Robbins and *The Tokyo–Montana Express* by Richard Brautigan'. *American Book Review*, 3, 3 (March–April 1981), p. 14.
Tanner, Tony. In *City of Words*, pp. 393, 406–15. New York: Harper & Row, 1971.